8-Week Depression Relief Workbook

—8-WEEK—
Depression
Relief
WORKBOOK

Evidence-Based Strategies
to Manage Your Symptoms

CYNTHIA V. CATCHINGS,
LCSW-S, LCSWC, CMHIMP, CFTP

ROCKRIDGE
PRESS

First Rockridge Press trade paperback edition 2022

Rockridge Press and the Rockridge Press logo are trademarks or registered trademarks of Callisto Media Inc. and/or its affiliates in the United States and other countries and may not be used without written permission.

For general information on our other products and services, please contact our Customer Care Department within the United States at (866) 744-2665, or outside the United States at (510) 253-0500.

Paperback ISBN: 978-1-63878-158-5 | eBook ISBN: 978-1-63878-400-5

Manufactured in the United States of America

Interior and Cover Designer: Stephanie Mautone
Art Producer: Maya Melenchuk
Production Editor: Holland Baker
Production Manager: Jose Olivera

All images used under license © Designdell/Creative Market. Author photo courtesy of Nicole Gates.

10 9 8 7 6 5 4 3 2 1 0

To all who wonder if they will feel better one day; to my mother, who has allowed depression to visit but never stay; and to my father, who never shared he was depressed.

Contents

Introduction

Welcome to a therapeutic journey we will take together for the next eight weeks! I am thrilled to share this workbook with you. During this time, we will work as a team. You will learn more about your feelings, depression, evidence-based therapy (EBT), and how to create a more enjoyable life through readings and guided activities.

My name is Cynthia Catchings. I am a psychotherapist, licensed clinical social worker-supervisor, certified family trauma professional, certified mental health integrative medicine professional, and professor who has helped hundreds of clients change their lives and reach their goals. For the past thirteen years, I have assisted individuals in learning to deal with depressive symptoms through therapy and education. I have traveled to over thirty countries to understand how individuals confront emotional issues and find solutions to their problems, including sadness and depression. This has allowed me to gather and share valuable information to help others.

As a therapist, I have worked with many individuals struggling with depression. Typically, during our first sessions, I identify the type of therapy that would be most beneficial for my client. I use cognitive behavioral therapy (CBT) most often due to its success rates and how clients respond to the therapeutic treatment. However, patients sometimes need a complement to CBT, so I started incorporating other EBT models to help, mainly with depression. As I began to include some of the information and activities you will see here, my clients responded well. Thanks to the combination of therapies, clients would often share how they felt happier and used the skills to fight the depressive symptoms in between sessions. That was fantastic!

As with any type of therapy, it can be challenging to reach your goals. You may have to remind yourself to work on your workbook and reflect on past, present, and future issues. However, you will not be doing that alone; I will be with you during this healing process. You can trust me and the advice provided in this workbook. Our goals are the same: to learn more about depression, its effects, and how to cope with it using tools and skills. You'll allocate some time every day to complete this workbook, and I will provide you with the tools and strategies to heal and move forward. So, get ready to spend some time with me in a safe and private place where you will reflect, heal, and create the life you truly want to live.

How to Use This Book

This workbook was written with you in mind and organized into two parts. Part 1 is an introduction to depression and the evidence-based approach to therapy. Part 2 is an eight-week program designed to reduce and manage symptoms of depression. Each week will include eight exercises: a check-in at the beginning, a reflection at the end, and six exercises in the middle to practice the concepts. You will also encounter affirmations, quick tip sidebars, and key takeaways to reflect, practice, and create change that will result in fewer depressive symptoms.

The workbook is a simple yet powerful tool intended to be completed linearly, with each week building on the prior week. Each "week" can be completed at your leisure but should be completed within a seven-day span. Keep your book in a private but accessible place, like your nightstand. Set a time of day to read and write and have an alternative time in case something comes up. For example, you can opt to write before going to bed, but if one day that is not possible, your alternative time can be in the morning before work or when you're unwinding after dinner. If possible, write in a place where you are alone and free from interruptions. Give yourself the necessary time to work on each activity. This is your opportunity to share, learn new skills, heal, and be yourself.

This book is intended for those with mild to moderate depression, not clinical or severe depression. In chapter 1, you will find a depression checklist to assess how your symptoms classify you. Although those individuals with severe depression can find valuable information in this book, I encourage them to contact a medical or mental health professional. Either one of these experts can help you select the best treatment plan. For those of you with mild to moderate symptoms, remember that this workbook is not a replacement for seeking treatment for depression. If symptoms of depression begin to cause serious distress or affect your ability to cope with home life, work life, or other people, you should seek treatment from a mental health professional. You can find local resources through FindTreatment.SAMHSA.gov. There is no shame in seeking help! It is essential to have a physician, dentist, and therapist to ensure that our health is in optimal condition. Holistic health is all about body, mind, and spirit.

Finally, keep in mind that you are in control, and you only have to dedicate a few minutes a day to this book during the next eight weeks. I will be walking next to you as you experience transformational improvement and overall well-being during this process of inner growth and healing.

PART I

Before You Start

Starting a new project can be daunting, but it gets easier once you begin. Working on this book is no exception. As mentioned earlier, each week builds on the previous week, and you will need to complete an activity every day. If you need a reminder, set an alarm or a notification on your phone. Next to your book, have a couple of pens or pencils and work in a well-lit area where you feel comfortable. Remember that you will benefit from your work, so it is worth the effort. You are worth it, so let's start our journey together!

1
Understanding Depression

Depression is more than sadness. It is a feeling that hurts, making it difficult to get out of bed, hard to eat, and challenging to socialize or stay active. Depression is not an emotion that quickly passes. It typically lingers, affecting us in different ways. That is precisely what makes it different from sadness or grieving. People sometimes ask me what depression is or what it feels like. The easiest way to explain it is by asking them if they have ever lost a loved one. Think about the heartache, pain, inability to do daily activities, intermittent crying spells, and deep sorrow they felt when that person left. That is what depression can feel like times ten, every day. There is no break. The intensity and range of symptoms will vary for each person, but in the end, it is painful and disruptive to all.

I dedicate time to myself each day to heal, grow, and feel better. I deserve this time.

What Is Depression?

Depression is a mood disorder characterized by an ongoing loss of interest and feeling of sadness, which can interfere with daily functioning. The severe sadness can prevent people from enjoying their everyday activities. But before we delve into a clinical description of depression, it is essential to highlight that every case is different. Those suffering can best explain what it feels like.

Depression can typically result from a combination of an individual's genetics (nature), life experiences (nurture), and psychological and biochemical factors. Unless there is a good record of the person's life and experiences, it is difficult to find a clear cause. According to the National Alliance on Mental Illness, individuals of all ethnic and socioeconomic backgrounds experience depression. A common myth is that depression is always inherited. According to Choose Mental Health, a person is predisposed to depression if it runs in the family; however, it will not always present in every family member if one family member had it.

Other factors at play in depression include an individual's brain wiring and their experiences with and response to trauma, along with how informed or ready the individual is to use tools to rewire the brain.

In scientific terms, depression is caused by the disruption of homeostatic mechanisms (regulators of our moods or emotions) that control synaptic plasticity (how effectively two neurons communicate with each other), resulting in disorder and loss of synaptic connections (learned information between neurons) in mood and emotion circuitry. Neurotransmitters involved in depression include norepinephrine, dopamine, and serotonin.

In simpler terms, neurons or nerve cells are responsible for "talking" among themselves, so we can do the things we need to do. To regulate our moods, and accomplish any activities or goals, we need neurons to communicate effectively. Depression may be caused by the disruption or loss of this crucial communication. More research is needed to understand all the factors involved in depression. Regardless of the underlying mechanisms, what's most important now is finding ways to manage depression.

Types of Depression

There are different types of depression. Knowing their names keeps us informed and can quiet our mind if we are concerned about what's wrong with us. For example, think of when you feel sick and go to doctor after doctor until you finally get an answer: Knowing what is wrong can provide relief and hopefully a plan of action. That same clarity can come from knowing our type of depression. However, here is a caveat: Mental health providers do not like to label clients unless those labels can inform our treatment plan. The following sections include information about types of depression. I invite you to use them for educational purposes only.

MAJOR DEPRESSION

Clinical depression, or major depressive disorder (MDD), is a mental health disorder included in the fifth edition of the *Diagnostic and Statistical Manual of Mental Disorders*, the most current, comprehensive resource for clinical practice used by researchers and mental health clinicians.

Major depression is typified by anhedonia, or a loss of interest in activities, which causes considerable impairment in daily life. In someone suffering from MDD, a depressed mood is experienced most of the time for most days of the week for over two weeks. By severe impairment, we mean inability to get out of bed, not showering or brushing teeth, and being absent from work or school, sometimes without notifying others. As with other types of depression, it is believed to be caused by a combination of psychological, biological, and situational issues that cause stress.

The persistent loss of interest, sadness, weight changes, and worthlessness that characterize major depression can lead to other behavioral and physical symptoms, including changes in energy, anger, appetite, sleep, self-esteem, concentration, or daily behavior. This type of depression can also be associated with suicidal thoughts or suicidal ideation (SI). The most common type of treatment is psychotherapy, medication, or a combination of the two.

PERSISTENT DEPRESSIVE DISORDER

Persistent depressive disorder (PDD) is defined as a long-running, low mood. Also known as dysthymia or chronic major depression, this type of depression is sometimes overlooked or misunderstood due to its diagnostic criteria, which is constantly evolving.

Before, PDD was listed as a personality disorder, which implied it was a perma-nent diagnosis. However, it is now much better conceptualized as a temporary state that can change.

PDD can be diagnosed by a mental health professional if the individual pres-ents depressive symptoms that have lasted for two years or longer. Its name is used to describe two different conditions that were known before as dysthymia (mild persistent depression) and chronic major depression. Please note that the latter is different from MDD in that it presents in episodes, is not chronic, and varies in intensity.

Some of the symptoms of PDD are sleeping too much or not sleeping, changes in appetite, low self-esteem, negative thinking, concentration problems, tiredness, hopelessness, and like some of my clients say, "feeling just meh." These individuals can function and complete daily activities, but they are just going through the motions.

SEASONAL AFFECTIVE DISORDER

Seasonal affective disorder (SAD) is a mood disorder in which individuals experi-ence depressive symptoms around the same time every year, typically during the fall and winter months, according to the Mayo Clinic. However, there may be varia-tions since SAD is also prevalent in areas where climates have less sunlight during certain times of the year. Some people can quickly identify this disorder because as soon as the weather changes or the holidays are around the corner, they start to experience symptoms.

Some of my clients have shared that they had never experienced depressive symptoms, but when they moved to a new city, where the days were shorter, and the sky was frequently cloudy, they started to feel down, sad, and even depressed. Although it is easy for me to recognize the symptoms, for some clients, it is not, so we have to work on education, including learning about tools to combat the SAD they are experiencing.

Some of the typical symptoms of SAD include sadness, depression, fatigue, social withdrawal, crying spells, and hopelessness. Treatment includes phototherapy/light therapy, weighted blankets, talk therapy, and medications.

MANIC DEPRESSION

This type is listed last not because it's not important but because it is com-monly misdiagnosed as depression. Manic depression is now known as bipolar disorder (BD). The new name was introduced during the third revision of the

DSM-5 in the 1980s. At that time, psychiatrists agreed to substitute the term "manic-depressive" because "manic" frequently led people to describe those with this condition as "maniacs," a label that contributed to judgment and stigma.

Those that are diagnosed with BD experience highs and lows. Instead of being sad, they experience depression and mania in no particular order. So, we observe individuals experiencing mood swings that range from depressive lows to manic highs.

Manic episodes include symptoms such as loss of touch with reality, erratic decision-making, reduced need for sleep, and grandiosity. Conversely, depressive episodes include symptoms such as lack of motivation, no energy, loss of interest in daily activities, guilt, low self-esteem, racing thoughts, risky behaviors, and anger. These episodes may last from days to months at a time and are sometimes also associated with suicidal ideation.

Bipolar disorder is broken down into two different diagnoses: bipolar I and bipolar II. The first type includes those people that have had a manic episode followed or preceded by a depressive episode. These individuals experience more depressive episodes than those diagnosed with bipolar II. A bipolar II diagnosis can be given when a person has had a hypomanic episode (an extreme change in mood) and a depressive episode but has not experienced high mania.

The particular cause of BD isn't known, but it is thought that a combination of chemistry, genetics, and environment may play a role. Lifelong treatment usually involves a combination of medications and psychotherapy.

Quick Tip: Using the Right Words

SITUATION: You learned that getting a diagnosis can be helpful in some instances but detrimental in others. Mental health issues carry a stigma that you have the power to end if you educate yourself and those around you.

QUICK TIP: In the same way that you would not say "He is diabetes" or "She is COVID-19," you should not label someone as "bipolar." Instead, it would be more appropriate to say, "They are diagnosed with or have bipolar disorder." Diagnosis is not identity. You experience depression but will never *be* it!

How Depression Manifests

Depression manifests in so many ways that sometimes it's challenging to recognize it. I've worked with clients who talk about signs such as lack of interest, canceling plans at the last minute, or experiencing crying spells. However, others have different symptoms that some people do not associate with depression. These include anger, road rage, stealing, absenteeism from work or school, and lying.

Others talk about discomfort in the chest—not sadness, but a hole, an emptiness. Scientifically, the most recognized symptoms are low energy, trouble with sleep, fatigue, loss of appetite, concentration problems, and aches that don't go away.

LOSS OF INTEREST

Earlier, we discussed anhedonia, or loss of interest in things you used to enjoy or complete loss of interest in everything, even things you did not care for much before. Although one might view anhedonia as almost like a form of depression, it is a symptom, and it can directly affect depression. And although it is a core symptom of major depressive disorder, it can be a symptom of other mental health issues as well.

So, what is the relationship between loss of interest and depression? Basically, depression creates a vicious cycle: The depression causes a loss of interest, which reduces activities and social interactions, producing negative thoughts that *further* reduce interest. Imagine running inside a wheel without being able to stop and get out. That is how loss of interest affects and is affected by depression. The more depressed you are, the more you lose interest in something. Activities such as journaling and worksheets can help end this negative cycle.

ANXIETY AND STRESS

Anxiety and stress are so related to depression that we could think of them as cousins. Although they are different mental health disorders, they can get together, interact at different levels, and leave when least expected. I introduce their relationship as "family" because they are very close. Still, they cannot be described as siblings because they are not always in the same house, but they come and visit just like relatives often do. According to the Anxiety and Depression Association of America, 50 percent of those diagnosed with depression also experience an anxiety disorder.

Stress and anxiety are affected by depression due to the frequent negative thoughts that create a dependent cycle. When depressed, a person tends to focus on the negative, over-worrying about what has not happened. For example, a depressed person might think that there is no point in calling in sick. They have no energy or interest and stay in bed feeling defeated. Later, the same negative thinking pattern brings anxiety about losing their job or not being able to pay their bills. The stress of being even more behind with work kicks in, and the depression cycle reappears.

UNCONTROLLABLE EMOTIONS

Uncontrollable emotions include crying, anger, frustration, negativity, and so on. The more depressed we are, the more these tend to happen, and the more unstable our moods become.

Emotional dysregulation is a concept we use to describe any emotional responses that are not regulated effectively. These responses are not accepted within the traditional range of emotional reactions. Emotional dysregulation is typically known as "mood swings." A good example is when a person is crying for some time and minutes later acts irritated or upset. Those around the person can be surprised by these reactions and suspect something is wrong with the person—without understanding that depression is the cause.

As you can see, depression has many causes and symptoms. The key is to remember that most physical and mental symptoms of depression also *reinforce* the depression. Although this can create a repeating cycle, we can learn to slow down the wheel and enjoy some periods of peace and tranquility.

DEPRESSION CHECKLIST

The following checklist helps you understand which type or level of depression you might have, but it is not a diagnostic tool. Talk to a professional if you have any questions or concerns. Check off each item you've experienced and write down its duration.

☐ Loss of interest or pleasure in activities ___

☐ Guilt ___

☐ Feeling tired ___

☐ Worthlessness ___

☐ Suicidal thoughts ___

☐ Restlessness ___

You might be experiencing major depression if you marked five or more of these symptoms, but only if you have had them most days for two weeks or longer.

☐ Change in appetite

☐ Disturbances

☐ Trouble concen-
   trating

☐ Unwillingness to
   make decisions

☐ Lack of energy

☐ Hopelessness

☐ Low self-esteem

☐ No interest in
   social gatherings

If you marked a minimum of five of these symptoms and have felt depressed for two years or longer, you might have persistent depressive disorder.

☐ Increased sleep

☐ Loss of interest in
   activities

☐ Social withdrawal

☐ Hopelessness

☐ Fatigue

☐ Decreased sex
   drive

☐ Weight gain

☐ Inability to focus

Seasonal affective disorder can also occur during the spring or summer. If you selected at least five of the items from this list, you might be experiencing symptoms of SAD.

☐ Mania

☐ Depressive mood

☐ Mood swings

☐ Talkativeness

☐ Irritability

☐ Racing thoughts

☐ Decreased need
   for sleep

☐ Grandiosity

☐ Thinking everyone is
   too slow

☐ Impulsivity

If you marked at least seven items, there is a significant possibility that you might be dealing with one of the bipolar disorder types.

   NOTE: Bipolar I disorder is a manic-depressive disorder that can be present with and without psychotic episodes. Bipolar II disorder presents depressive and manic episodes that alternate and are typically milder.

Key Takeaways

- Depression typically results from a combination of an individual's genetics (nature), events (nurture), or psychological and biochemical factors, and its symptoms vary from person to person, so everyone's experience differs.

- Self-work is a good and recommended way to treat depression, and that starts by educating ourselves about this condition.

- There is plenty to be hopeful about since there are many effective ways to treat depression.

- Depression is a serious condition that requires psychoeducation, perseverance, and patience. You finished this chapter, which tells us that you are ready to continue because you have all three.

- There are different ways to treat depression, and you can select the best for you. EBT is a combination of effective modalities for treating depression. You will start learning about it in the next chapter, so be ready to explore what it is all about.

2
The Approach

You have learned about the various types of depression and how they can be experienced differently. You know that depression's symptoms, like fatigue and a persistent feeling of loss, can lead to diverse behavioral and physical problems. Although depression is not something that can be cured, shaken off, or thrown away, you can learn to live with it. Learning to deal with what you feel is vital to decreasing your symptoms. To do that, you need to learn tools and skills. This chapter includes information about the combination of therapies known as evidence-based therapy that can help you do that. It is crucial to remember that this is not a single type of therapy but a mix of different proven approaches, including cognitive behavioral therapy (CBT), dialectical behavior therapy (DBT), and more.

All I can do is my best, and if
I have the right tools and skills,
I believe I will succeed.

An Intro to Evidence-Based Therapy

When some people think about therapy, the first thing they think about is an older gentleman with a white beard, smoking a cigar, sitting in front of a client who is reclined on a couch. Fortunately, that is not how therapy looks these days. With increased research and knowledge, we have more effective types of therapy and more diverse mental health professionals. That is precisely what evidence-based therapy, also known as evidence-based treatment, is all about. The principles of evidenced-based practice are that every treatment decision must be based on research that demonstrates the effectiveness of that specific therapy, and that treatment progress must be measured in consistent ways.

WHAT IS EBT?

Evidence-based therapy is better known in the professional mental health circles as evidence-based practice because it combines any type of therapy that has been scientifically demonstrated to be valid or effective. EBT adheres to psychological techniques and approaches based on scientific evidence. It is also called best practice. One of the things therapists like the most about this practice is that it incorporates the preferences of the client or patient. For example, with any EBT, the therapist educates the client about the treatment approach and its benefits. The therapist also invites the client to try different types of EBT through questions, activities, and exercises and once again asks the client to voice what is working and what is not. As a clinician, I explain to my clients that I use CBT and later incorporate other modalities as needed, but they are always in control. I walk by their side until they are ready to run alone. You can think of EBT as a group of therapy practices researched, accepted, and proven to be effective by mental health professionals.

TYPES OF EBT

Although EBT has various modalities, I want to present a few that are most common nowadays. These are not listed in any particular order, and there is some overlap between them, as you will see.

CBT

Cognitive behavioral therapy (CBT) is the most used therapy in the United States. When I meet with fellow mental health professionals, we discuss our preferred and current modalities. We may have different approaches, but CBT is always our common denominator. CBT is based on helping you change your thought patterns and actions in the present. In other words, change your thoughts to change your actions. CBT enables you to address your issues without worrying too much about what happened to you in the past. You work alone or with your therapist in the here and now.

Most importantly, CBT is educational and goal oriented. You learn the skills to feel better and select your own goals. For example, you learn to identify emotions, reframe, think positively, and journal, and you often have homework consisting of activities or worksheets. It also uses a variety of strategies, such as guided imagery, role-playing, and talking to your depression or anxiety.

MBCT

Mindfulness-based cognitive therapy is based on cognitive behavioral therapy, but more than written activities, you use mindfulness and meditation techniques to consciously observe and identify your thoughts and feelings. The main idea is to do that without judging yourself, allowing these practices to help you free your mind.

ACT

Acceptance and commitment therapy is a relatively newer therapy that has been proven to decrease depression and has gained more respect and followers within the last twenty years. It focuses on working with thoughts and feelings that over-whelm you and your sense of well-being. It helps you overcome internal battles with emotional pain while committing to what matters in your life through values (things you like or enjoy doing), acceptance, and commitment. Basically, the client accepts the depression and, without trying to ignore or avoid the symptoms, commits to concentrate on their life-affirming values.

MINDFULNESS

Mindfulness is a practice that can be used within the three types of therapy we have just reviewed. It is not a type of therapy but one of the most powerful tools for the EBT approaches. It invites you to live in the present and not allow negative emotions to affect you.

Benefits of EBT

Evidence-based treatments offer mental health practitioners, integrative teams, and clients many benefits. For clinicians and their practices to be ethical, it is necessary that they are guided by current and relevant scientific data. Hence the importance of EBT. If something has not been demonstrated or proven to work, it may raise concerns among practitioners and clients. In the same way that a person would not take a medication that has not been approved by the FDA, someone should not agree to participate in a therapeutic session if the approach has not been researched and approved. It would be a non-evidence-based practice.

An excellent way to better understand the benefits of EBT is by looking at reputable and trusted organizations that use it. On its website, the Department of Veterans Affairs (VA) states that it is committed to providing the best possible care to veterans, and that commitment includes making evidence-based therapies available to veterans within their health care system. If the VA, as a reputable agency, trusts EBT and its best practices, other professionals feel comfortable using and implementing it, making it even more evidence based.

But how about the benefits for the clients, you may wonder. Recently, a client asked me about cognitive behavioral therapy (CBT). As mentioned before, CBT falls under the EBT umbrella. "How do you know it works or will benefit me?" he said. My answer was automatic since I had known the answer for years: I know it works because I have seen it change my patients' lives for the best and because it has been scientifically proven to be effective through peer-reviewed research. Even the VA uses it to help our heroes. EBT is effective for many reasons: First, it reduces negative symptoms while promoting recovery and improving the quality of life of those being treated. Second, it is goal oriented. That means that mental health professionals and clients work together to identify and reach the goals that the client selected with the therapist's guidance. Third, it is empowering. Clients learn the necessary skills by completing activities, exercises, and readings that help them live with fewer symptoms and be more in control of their lives. Furthermore, the treatment is relatively quick since the results start to be visible within six to twelve sessions. Finally, EBT has lasting benefits even after the treatment ends because the client becomes informally trained in these therapies after obtaining tools and learning skills.

Quick Tip: Mental Gym

THE SITUATION: EBT is a highly accepted and used approach because the therapist and the client work together to create a treatment plan that the client follows. The skills or tools can be learned independently with the help of a book, workbook, or in therapy.

QUICK TIP: The goal is the same for you to be able to learn how to handle negative thoughts and emotions and to use what has been learned to decrease depressive symptoms. Pay attention to your thoughts frequently. When you find yourself thinking negatively, stop, and reframe as many times as needed. You are not looking for immediate change but rather training your brain to think positively.

EBT and Depression

Mental health professionals view EBT and depression like peas in a pod. EBT effectively reduces symptoms, giving hope to those that have been depressed for months. When clients start telling us that they feel better, we know it is working. The varied treatments that fall under EBT explore the relationships and disconnections between emotions and thoughts, helping the client with their depressive symptoms. For example, CBT focuses on changing the negative or unwanted depressive thoughts and behaviors in order to improve actions, mood, and well-being in general. As you can see, it is based on changing your thoughts to be able to change your emotions. EBT provides you with tools that you get to practice or implement for as long as needed.

My clients frequently bring up the topic of feeling better and ending depression for good. Common questions they ask me are *Does therapy really work? Am I going to feel better one day? Will my depression ever go away?* Of course therapy works! That is precisely what EBT proves: It makes a difference in people's lives. My answer to the second question is yes; the evidence-based work we do with our clients allows us to say that, although every person is different, their symptoms will improve as long as they do the work. And to the third question, I answer no because depression is a mental health issue that never goes away, but we can learn to control it thanks to EBT.

EBT has been effective in the treatment of depression because it teaches you to heal yourself rather than covering the pain with a bandage. You learn to break down your problems into different parts. You may be invited to write; journaling allows you to share and identify your emotions, feelings, and thoughts. You also learn to observe your feelings, ideas, and behaviors. By doing that, you can see how they are connected and how they alleviate or worsen your depressive symptoms. Most importantly, EBT is effective because you will never be asked to do anything you would not like to do. You are always in control and go at your own pace.

Key Takeaways

- EBT includes several types of therapies, approaches, and practices. These include CBT, ACT, MBCT, and mindfulness.

- Skills and tools in therapy refer to activities and practices, including breathing techniques, worksheets, and reframing, to name a few. These can be learned from a workbook and/or reinforced by a mental health professional.

- EBT benefits clients during and after treatment since they become "trained to help themselves."

- Typically, a client using EBT can expect to see results within six to twelve sessions.

- EBT allows clients to choose their own therapy goals and work on them at their pace.

PART II

Start Your Journey

Some people wonder when the best time is to start a journey. I would say the best time to start is today—even if you don't feel completely ready for the journey. How many times have you said, *I will do it tomorrow*, only to say the same thing when tomorrow comes? So, today, let's begin a new chapter. You are the captain of this journey. Each exercise you'll complete here will teach you to better control depressive symptoms and target different goals. You've got this!

Setting Your Baseline

This week, you will learn about tools, skills, and goals. Tools refer to any idea, activity, or practice. So, think of them as something you will keep in a handy tool kit to control depression. These tools may not always be tangible or visible, but you will be able to access them as needed whenever you want. Skills are hands-on activities that you learn to practice and eventually become natural reactions or responses. Goals are the things you want to accomplish. If you do your homework by using the tools and skills you will learn here, you can expect to see your goals come to fruition.

Some tools and skills you will cover are ways to decrease negative thinking, using your senses and imagination to curb depression, getting to know yourself, and taking positive and practical steps.

I am in control of my thoughts and emotions, and I can create change in my life.

CHECKING IN

Activities, commitments, and responsibilities can feel like heavy burdens if you are depressed. Maybe you have tried to find ways to reduce the effects that those "burdens" cause, perhaps by watching TV, walking around the house, or taking a nap. However, sometimes you may not have the time and luxury to do any of those things because you have a project that is due or you have to attend a work or family event. There is a quick and easy way to help yourself when that happens.

Breathing comes naturally, and you might see it as a simple body function. But when you are intentional about it, you can harness it to calm your body and reduce stress, anxiety, or depressive symptoms. The easiest way to do this is called 4-7-8 breathing. In this method, also known as the relaxing breathing technique, you breathe in for four seconds, hold your breath for seven seconds, and exhale for eight seconds. Try it, repeat it three times, then save it in your tool kit for future use. Reflect on your experience here.

Where Are You Now?

When did you last ask yourself how you were feeling, or did a scan of your emotions to see if any symptoms were present? These practices help you understand where you are in your current relationship with depression.

For example, imagine you woke up with a sore throat and cough this morning. You take a few minutes to check your temperature and look for other symptoms, like body aches, sneezing, or chills. Those few minutes you take to do a body scan make all the difference. Either they give you peace of mind—you know it may be just allergies or a cold—or you grab your phone so you can schedule an appointment to get tested as soon as possible. When you take some time to observe, you allow yourself to evaluate, recognize, and deal with your symptoms.

In the same way, taking the time to check your emotional state is essential. If you wake up feeling down or fatigued but do not perform a body scan, you might be allowing the depression to extend its visit. Taking the time to observe and check in with your emotions enables you to decide what to do next.

Depression can be an unwanted feeling, a burden, or even something we know comes and goes. What truly makes the difference is how we view, accept, and deal with it. What is your current relationship with depression? Are you feeling it? Did it just leave, or did it go away a couple of days ago? What do you do when it arrives?

Most importantly, how do you take care of yourself when it is present? Let's go back to the example I talked about earlier. If you had a cold, you might rest, take something to feel better, or eat a good soup. How about when you feel depressed? Do you pamper yourself in the same way? Do you eat good foods or find a nice place to recharge?

Now that you have reflected on those questions, hopefully you see a clearer picture of your relationship with depression. Throughout this week, you'll complete exercises that assess depression's severity, duration, and impact on your daily functioning.

Quick Tip: Feeling Depressed

THE SITUATION: Depression is an illness that can negatively affect how you act or feel when in company or alone. You start feeling sad, angry, or moody. You ask yourself, *Why do I feel this way?* You want to shake the feelings off but can't make yourself do it. You have physical symptoms and want to know how to stop them.

QUICK TIP: Sit down and spend a few minutes scanning your body and emotions to evaluate where they come from. Take a deep breath. Then exhale, imagining how you take the negative feelings out of your body.

OBSERVING YOUR THOUGHTS

The first step toward assessing your depression is to become an observer of negative thoughts without attaching to them. The mind immediately wants to identify with these thoughts and make them a new pattern of thinking. This is called getting obsessed with your thoughts. The more that you practice recognizing these thoughts as an observer, the easier it will be to let them go.

This activity invites you to recognize the situations that make you obsess over your thoughts and the responses that you typically provide.

You will start by using the following rating scale to rate your depression **before and after the activity**:

0	1	2	3	4	5	6	7
Nonexistent	Minimal	Slight	Mild	Moderate	Much Higher	Very High	Extreme

Read the following questions and answer them in the spaces provided. After you complete it, read your answers, and reflect on them. Now that you know more about how your mind works and how you react, you can observe how you respond when you find yourself in similar situations in the future.

CONTINUED ▶

OBSERVING YOUR THOUGHTS CONTINUED ▸

WHAT SITUATIONS DOES YOUR MIND CREATE THAT MAKE YOU FEEL OBSESSED?	WHAT DOES YOUR OBSESSIVE MIND TELL YOU?	WHAT DO YOU DO TO STOP OBSESSING?
Ex: I got in trouble at work or school.	Ex: I am not good at what I do.	Ex: This is an opportunity to improve, not to dwell on it.

REFLECTIONS

MY DEPRESSION SCRIPT

While completing the previous exercise, you practiced letting go of your negative thoughts to stop overthinking. In the following activity, you will work on recognizing how long you have experienced negative thinking and depressive symptoms, how they make you feel, and what you can do to change the pattern. As you combine both skills, you will have more opportunities to learn and use other tools and aptitudes.

Fill in the following prompts. When you are done, slowly read your answers aloud to yourself.

I started noticing I felt depressed when

Some of my depressive symptoms are

I remember having negative thoughts since I

When I am having those unwanted thoughts, I feel

Holding on to these thoughts is unhelpful because

When I do not let the negative thoughts go, I notice that

That may cause me suffering due to

And I notice that my negative thinking affects me because

What I can do to stop these thoughts is

How do you feel after reading your answers? Is there something else you can do to reduce your depressive symptoms?

Where Do You Want to Be?

Depression is a complicated condition. Its many levels and symptoms can affect people in unique ways. Depending on its severity and where you find yourself in life, it can make it challenging for you to look at the future, stay motivated, and think about success. Although it has been established that depression may not be eliminated entirely, it is necessary to know that it can be managed.

Thinking about what success would look like for you, what would you like to accomplish with this workbook? Be generous with your wishes or wants. I have clients that tell me I just want to wake up and have the energy to start a new day. Others want to fill that void inside them that prevents them from experiencing happiness. Some just want to have the energy and interest to go out and meet with family or friends. How about you? Where do you want to be emotionally at the end of this book? Remember, you can list as many things as you wish.

Thinking about staying motivated, what could keep you interested? Think about three to five things that motivate you and write them down to help you during this journey. Sometimes it can be challenging to create a list. An excellent way to do it is to think about what you enjoyed or liked to do before feeling depressed. You may not be able to remember a time when you did not feel depressed. Anhedonia, also known as an inability to feel pleasure, is a typical symptom of depression. If you have experienced it for a long time, you may have difficulty thinking about things that motivate you now, recently, or in the past. If that is the case, try using the following affirmation: *There is a light at the end of the tunnel; these activities will help me get the tools to reduce my depressive symptoms so I can better cope.*

Throughout this journey, remind yourself about the importance of staying motivated. Initially, you may want to use reminders, but the more you practice, the easier it'll be for you to see this workbook as a positive routine. Maybe you'll enjoy the exercises so much that you'll look forward to completing the next one. Whatever your motivation is, remember: You're in control!

Quick Tip: Letting Negative Thoughts Go

THE SITUATION: You're at home and feel depressed. As you wait for a loved one that was supposed to be back home an hour ago, you call and text them. No response. You cry or feel angry while worrying about something happening to them. You ask yourself, *Why are they not communicating with me? Did something happen to them?*

QUICK TIP: While walking around the room and taking deep breaths, think about more positive reasons why they're late. If that's not possible, sit and write the reasons down. Maybe they have no battery on their phone. Perhaps they are in the middle of a conversation and can't answer the phone.

MY PERSONAL JOURNEY

Your story is unique and special; your set of experiences has shaped your own journey. You find yourself where you are due to circumstances and choices but also genetics. Some situations have been pleasant, and others have been problematic. When you start to complete this exercise, include both types of experiences. If you can remember what was happening when you started to feel depressed for the first time, add it and circle it or put a check mark next to it. If you cannot remember, use examples of times when you felt depressive symptoms (for example, *when my friends left* or *when I lost my job*). This activity allows you to see which situations have been significant or pivotal in your life.

Remember, you will include the positive and the not-so-positive and will circle or put a check mark next to the specific situation(s) that may have caused or contributed to your depression.

CONTINUED ▶

List five key moments that illustrate your journey and be as descriptive as you can. The more detail you include, the better. *Ex: When my grandmother died.*

How have these personal experiences influenced your journey? If you find it challenging to narrow down important moments, give yourself a few minutes and then write them down. *Ex: I felt lonely and started to experience depression.*

WHAT'S THAT HAPPY TUNE?

Your thoughts dictate your actions or behaviors. They have more power over you than you realize because you constantly hear them. When you have negative thoughts, it's like listening to sad music, and your app always plays the same songs.

In this exercise, you'll list some of the thoughts that affect you and then move to create a more fun list of things that change your mood and thinking process. Again, this will help you observe your negative thoughts and mindfully use music to shift the tune to change those thoughts and behaviors.

Create a list of situations that make you have negative thoughts. For example, being in traffic, someone ghosting you, and so on. When you're done, think of songs that lift your spirit and write them down to listen to when needed.

When you are done, take a picture of your lists and save it on your phone or, if you have time, make a playlist you can use when needed. In the future, you can sing these songs or listen to your playlist when you want to feel more content.

SITUATIONS	SONGS

Goals

In my sessions, one of the most important moments I have with the client is when they set their goals. People can talk or cry, which is productive, but the moment they set goals, the therapeutic process becomes a reality, a commitment, and a chance for a new life. Stating your goals is crucial, but there must be purpose and intentionality behind it. If you only write your dreams and do not do anything about them, they will not become a reality.

Goals must be SMART for them to become a reality. This acronym refers to a method that helps people effectively reach their goals. It stands for:

Specific. *Your goals are well-defined and allow you to answer the who, what, when, why, and where.*

Ex: I'll start by looking at gyms in my area today because I want to get fit.

Measurable. *You can measure progress during the journey, which allows you to know when you'll reach your goals.*

Ex: I will use my watch or app to monitor my daily activity.

Achievable. *Your goals are attainable because you have the resources and skills to reach that goal.*

Ex: I have exercised before, I can pay for a gym membership, and I have time to go.

Relevant. *Your goals are important to you and have a purpose.*

Ex: I want to feel stronger and become fitter.

Time-bound. *Your goals typically have a deadline that you must meet.*

Ex: I have a marathon in six months.

When you use this model, you eliminate any confusion. In other words, you gain clarity. When you set these goals, you understand what you need to do and when you need it so you can achieve your outcome.

REWARDS

Rewards are a healthy component of staying motivated. To evaluate motivation during a session, I ask my clients, "How would you feel if you worked for a week or two or maybe a month, and at the end of it, you had not gotten paid?" Perhaps you would make a phone call. Maybe you would wait until the next business day to go in person and ask why you hadn't been paid. The majority respond, "I would not keep going!"

Depending on the job, pay is the motivator for most people. Without a reward, most people do not continue making an effort. The same applies to this journey. The reward doesn't have to be money. It can be eating your favorite meal or dessert or watching that movie you have been waiting for. It can even be a trip to the mall or the beach. Everyone has their own preferences to reward themselves and get inspired. What will yours be?

LOOKING FORWARD TO ACCOMPLISHING MY GOALS

Using tools like the one you are about to work with can make the goal-setting process easier. Although there are several ways to practice goal setting, only you can decide what works for you. This is a favorite worksheet for many people. It will help you see the process through a different lens.

Fill in the blanks and then enter the answers after each question or idea.

I want to accomplish these short- or long-term goals:

My expected accomplishing dates are ,

,

and .

These goals are important to me because

Here is how my goals are SMART:

Specific

_____

Measurable

_____

Achievable

_____

Relevant

_____

Time-bound

_____

_____

I will complete the following steps or actions to ensure I achieve my goals:

_____

_____

_____

I make a commitment with myself to reach these goals and will share them with a

person I trust and love, _____ ,

so I can share with them how I feel or how my work toward reaching my goals is going.

I commit to reaching my goals and not giving up.

QUIZ TIME

Before you end this chapter, you will practice with a quiz. It will show you how you think and process your thoughts.

Circle the number that applies to you.

0=Never, 1=Sometimes, 2=Frequently

1. I am practicing letting go of negative thoughts.

    0   1   2

2. I have some ideas about how to talk to myself to get motivated.

    0   1   2

3. Music, books, films, or other hobbies help me change my mood.

    0   1   2

4. I can develop some ideas to reward myself and stay motivated.

    0   1   2

5. I find myself more active or interested in things.

    0   1   2

RESULTS:

8–10: You are a pro! You are learning how to help yourself and not let negative or difficult situations affect you.

6–7: You know how to control some situations and use the skills you have learned.

3–5: You are on your way to learning how to manage your thinking process. Keep practicing!

0–2: Sometimes your mood is so low that it is difficult to see the tools and skills you possess to feel better. You may want to review some of the previous activities and look forward to completing the following exercises.

PAUSE AND REFLECT

Let's stop for a moment and take some time to reflect. What has called your attention the most from what you have read? Why do you think that is? Have you identified something that is present in your life?

Reflection is another part of the process. You can read or complete one of the exercises in this book, close it, and go on with your day, or you can take a few minutes and reflect on what you have covered. Both have their benefits. The first one gives you the opportunity to learn and move forward. The second one gives you the same but also invites you to process and think of ways to implement what you added to your tool kit.

Working at your own pace also makes a big difference in how you process what you have covered. Unlike attending a therapy session, working with a book like this one allows you to truly go at your speed. You decide if you want to give the book some time in the morning or at night, you can do the work daily, and you can go back and review the material from a previous day.

Key Takeaways

- Your mind plays tricks on you, making you overthink. Let it go!

- You are in control of what you think and how you behave.

- Hobbies, exercise, music, and other activities can be helpful to stop overthinking.

- Your goals have to be SMART.

- Practice gratitude and "thank your mind" for avoiding taking your thoughts too seriously.

WEEK 2

Defining Your Values

Congratulations on advancing to the next level! This week, you will focus on reinforcing the positive thinking you practiced a few days ago, and an exciting new topic will be introduced: defining your values. When it comes to values, you have the power to implement them to create change since they are what you want your life to be about or how you would like to be.

When was the last chance you had to do something interesting or fun that reflected your values? Sometimes you do things that reflect them even without thinking. For example, you can help someone carry their bags to their car at the grocery store. That act demonstrates the values of kindness, love, and gratitude. There are many values, and when you start defining yours, you will see how they are part of who and what you are.

My goals are aligned with my values, and I am true to them and the life they guide me to live.

CHECKING IN

As you may already know, your values are created by you and come directly from your desires. They're your positive labels or what you or others associate you with.

Some time ago, I worked with a person who wanted to travel around the world and see fifty countries before turning fifty. Everyone that knew this person imagined a world traveler when they heard their name. Fortunately, this individual accomplished their dream and continued working on different projects with different values, but that traveling marker was like a signature that no one forgot. Throughout your life, your values may change, but they'll help you grow, enjoy life, and be true to yourself as you build your desired world.

Now this is your turn to share more about the positive thinking you practiced last week and your values. Use the following space to write a letter to yourself answering these questions: What do you want to do with your time in this world, and what kind of person would you like to be? When you're done, read your letter to yourself.

Why Values?

When you were growing up, maybe you heard the word "values" at home or school. Perhaps your guardians or your teachers talked about being good or behaving well in school. Those values, also known as morals, were related to being a good person or citizen. The values we're talking about today are somewhat related but a little different. These are internal motivators that guide you in life; activities that give your life meaning, define, or describe you; or something you are known for or will be remembered for. Values differ from goals in that goals end once achieved.

Values are lifelong things we cherish. Values give your life purpose and meaning and help you decrease some depressive symptoms. Recently, I asked someone, *What are your values?* The person said cultures and learning. *Why?* I asked. The person immediately responded, *Because those things make me happy! I want to visit other lands, learn about cultures, and see where history happened.* Ding, ding, ding! That's what values are about: things that make you feel good.

DETERMINE YOUR VALUES

Values define how you would like to behave on an ongoing basis. They can be described as desired qualities of continuous action, or frequently chosen life directions. Therapists typically compare values to a compass because they provide you with direction and guide you throughout your journey.

To determine your values, you can think about what is truly important to you, the most essential, what gives your life meaning and purpose. For example, think about the answers to the following questions. What do you want your life to be about? What do you want to do that you cannot do because of the depression? The answers reflect your values.

Think about a friend you trust. What personal values or qualities would you share about yourself or talk about with them? For example, I want to learn to speak Italian (learning value), or I wish to laugh more often (happiness value).

If you haven't yet, soon you'll pick yours. Read the following sample. Then assign an importance level to each point, with 1 being not important and 10 being the most important. When you are done, look at those marked with 7 or above and reflect on why they are important to you:

- Acceptance: to accept myself and others.

- Beauty: to enjoy, appreciate, and cultivate beauty in myself and others.

- Compassion: to be kind to those who are suffering.

Quick Tip: Values Change

THE SITUATION: Last month, you were reading and feeling much better. The book was exciting, and you were really engaged. Staying busy and interested in the plot allowed you to get distracted and not think about your depression. Once you finished the book, the negative feelings return. You thought about getting another book, but you did not feel like reading anymore.

QUICK TIP: Values are not always the same. Since you are not interested in reading, look for other activities or values. Spend time listening to music, watching a funny or educational video, or starting a journal. What other ideas come to your mind to stay motivated and distracted based on your values?

CHECKING YOUR VALUES

As you already know, values are chosen life directions; activities that define you, describe you, or give your life meaning; or things you are known for or will be remembered for. To be able to follow and reflect your values, you need to know what they are. When you do not know them, you can still function and keep going, but life gets a little bit more complicated. To make your life simpler, you will start by taking a few minutes to think about your values. Then you can begin the following exercise.

Mark the values that are important to you. There is no minimum or maximum, so you can go over the list once or twice to make sure you mark all the ones that are important to you.

☐ Acceptance	☐ Excitement	☐ Love
☐ Assertiveness	☐ Fitness	☐ Mindfulness
☐ Beauty	☐ Flexibility	☐ Order
☐ Caring	☐ Freedom	☐ Patience
☐ Challenge	☐ Friendliness	☐ Power
☐ Compassion	☐ Gratitude	☐ Respect
☐ Cooperation	☐ Honesty	☐ Responsibility
☐ Creativity	☐ Humor	☐ Romance
☐ Curiosity	☐ Independence	☐ Self-care
☐ Equality	☐ Justice	☐ Trust
☐ Empathy	☐ Kindness	

What top five values from this list would you say are your favorite ones?

How do you practice those five on a daily basis?

EXPLORING A LITTLE MORE

You have been practicing creating change in your life by choosing and clarifying your values. To define your values, you also need to know who and what influences them. Before you can move on to other practices, you will continue sharing and practicing more until you identify and make the best use of your values.

When people's actions—or life in general—are not aligned with their values, they may experience difficulties, mood disorders, and negative thoughts and feelings that translate into depressive and sometimes destructive behaviors. So, take a few minutes to list the values of those who have influenced or still influence you and how you are truly following your values.

Ex: Love: Care about others, give words of affirmation.

Ex: Laughter: Watch funny movies, go to a comedy show, practice laughter yoga.

My parent's values:

1.

2.

3.

4.

A loved one's values:

1.

2.

3.

4.

My closest friend's values:

1.

2.

3.

4.

The values I am living by:

1.

2.

3.

4.

The values I would like to live by:

1.

2.

3.

4.

USING A HOLISTIC APPROACH TO CHOOSE YOUR VALUES

By now, you know that values are essential rules that you develop over time. Earlier, you checked the values that are important to you. Then you got to list those of people around you, seeing where your own values may come from or what they are. That last opportunity to clarify others' values was helpful to know who and what influences your own. You will get more specific this time.

Many therapists, including myself, value using a holistic approach. That means that we try to combine and promote our patient's physical, mental, and emotional well-being. Now you will use that same approach while completing this exercise. You will get a chance to work on values related to three common domains in life. Take as much time as you need to write your set of values related to each of the following three domains.

PHYSICAL	MENTAL	EMOTIONAL
Ex: Fitness, healthy eating, etc.	*Ex: Meditation, mindfulness*	*Ex: Share feelings with others.*

Values in Practice

It's essential to make time to live life according to your values. By doing so, you provide purpose and motivation, which aids in depression recovery. Here are some suggestions to live life according to your values.

Writing them down, as simple as that sounds, is the best way to start. Once you have them written down in front of you, then you can define them. For example, if you select *stability* as one of your values, define what stability means to you, how it can be accomplished, and what you may need to implement it.

Identifying what values are already present in your life is also useful. When they are showing up already, it is much easier to use them. Think about the value of traveling. If you're able to travel regularly or it is easy for you to take time off, the value is showing up. Another good example is peace. If you already take the opportunity to sit in your room and have a peaceful moment, the value is present.

LIVING YOUR VALUES

Go back and review your responses in the last section. You chose a value to implement. Now let's look at some examples to make it even easier. You will see some of the values mentioned in previous sections and some activities to fulfill each value. Imagine what you could accomplish if you tried one of those activities each week! It would be a game-changer if you added one of those activities to the weekly check-in exercise that you practice here at the beginning of each week.

Professional skills. *These refer to your life as a professional, student, or staying-at-home individual. Implementing examples are registering for a course, volunteering at a shelter, learning to decorate your home, or making repairs around the house.*

Relationships. *These refer to friendship, bonding, closeness, and intimacy. Implementing examples include going to places where you can meet people, calling your friends or visiting them, and spending time with your partner regularly. Also, taking care of family members by feeding them or taking them to a fun place.*

Self-care. *These values refer to your development as a human being, including good hygiene, exercise, nutrition, and sleep. Implementing examples include walks in the park, watching a good movie at home, taking a warm bath, getting a haircut, taking vitamins, taking time to be on our own, and completing workbooks like this one!*

As you can see, you need to be somewhat creative after you choose your values since knowing them is only a piece of the puzzle. You need to find ways to nourish those activities you choose to do and commit to them while giving yourself the time to become the person you want to be.

Quick Tip: Rumination

THE SITUATION: Lately, you've been experiencing mood changes. You sit on the bed and wonder why you feel depressed. Minutes later, you realize you've been there for a while. Knowing that you have things to do, you lay down and start ruminating. One negative thought leads to another. Once again, you tell yourself you have to finish something, but you close your eyes instead of getting up.

QUICK TIP: Using your values to your benefit is what it's all about. Think of financials, goal-reaching, or responsibility as values. Which of the three calls you the most and makes you get up and finish? Use that. You are stronger than any negative thoughts or depressive symptoms.

A GOOD LIFE

Have you ever met a person that thinks their life is almost perfect? Perhaps it is because their values are aligned. Once you align yours, you, too, will enjoy more of what you do, and your depressive symptoms will decrease. For this activity, you will have to be creative. You'll fill in the blanks to complete the story, thinking about how your life would be if you followed those values you would like to live by.

My life today is

I would like to incorporate more of those values I would like to live by such as

_____ and _____ .

That would allow me to feel _____ and do _____ ,

including _____ _____

_____

_____ .

If I live by those values, I will be able to _____

because _____ .

That can be achieved by _____ and with the help of

_____ , but most importantly by me keeping a

_____ and _____ attitude and

_____ my behaviors.

Take a moment to read the story to yourself. Are you happy with it, or do you need to modify something? How can you use that information to motivate you to get closer to your almost perfect life?

_____

_____

_____

_____

_____

_____

WHAT MY FRIENDS SEE

You know and easily recognize your values by now. You have also put them into practice. This next step is to consistently reconnect with those values. Although we select our own values, and others cannot or must not do it for us, others can still recognize them and look up to us in the same way we admire or respect those with aligned values.

It is obvious when someone feels confident and comfortable in their skin, which comes from the security of living a good life. This exercise will invite you to share what you think your friends see in you. Imagine you are celebrating your birthday five years from now. Your family and close friends give their speeches about you and how you have lived your life, a life aligned with your values.

What do you hear them say?

What values are constantly repeated or shared by them while they talk?

As you hear them speak about you, what makes you happy and proud?

Were there any values they did not mention that you think you live by? If so, list them here and why they are essential to you.

WHO DO YOU LOOK UP TO?

Everyone has people they look up to or admire. These individuals can be alive or not. In the case of those who are no longer living, maybe they made history during their time in this world, making others respect them. Those who are still present do extraordinary things that align with their values. Not surprisingly, if you dig a little deeper into the lives of those you admire, you'll find that their values seem to be somewhat connected with yours. In my case, I admire Socrates and Plato; both of them had an interest in the psyche or mind. They reflected and worked on learning about the intellect, or what they thought of as the soul. They also asked many questions to help themselves and others understand the human condition. Does that sound like a therapist to you?

I shared mine, so it is your turn to share yours. Name a person or two that you admire from the present or past. Why do you admire them? What do you think this person's values are? How many of those values do you share? What would you talk about or tell this person if you had the opportunity to meet with them in private?

PAUSE AND REFLECT

You have completed another week! So, it is now time to pause, review, and reflect on what you have learned these past days. Ask yourself the following questions, thinking about the material you covered: *When I merge myself with my values, I create an existence with meaningful directions. How easy or how difficult is it for me to select my values? Since my values come directly from my mind's and heart's desires, which values are the closest to me?*

While you identified your values and practiced how to use or benefit from them, you also learned that you are not obligated to keep a value, since you can change them. Ask yourself: *In what ways will I be able to recognize these changes and adapt or incorporate new values? Does working with values bring me happiness or joy?*

As you can imagine, enjoying what you do, not simply doing it as a responsibility, transforms your state of mind. You are selecting things that are important to you, being present, and designing part of your life. That is a huge accomplishment. You are becoming more in control day by day, and hopefully this momentum will continue every week. Good job!

Key Takeaways

- You can set goals based on your true values when you know what those values are.

- For goals to become a reality, you have to be flexible, as situations may change. This flexibility permits you to adapt to changes without losing the drive and commitment to follow your values.

- You can always take a moment to reexamine your actions and ensure they line up with your values and goals.

- Your values are a constant motivating force for your behaviors.

- All goals require you to stay motivated and committed to following what you care about, even when obstacles are present.

WEEK 3

Coming to Terms with Your Emotions

People are not always encouraged to get in touch with their emotions. Many people wear a smiling mask when they leave their house every morning, and no one knows how they truly feel inside. Sometimes not even they know what is going on internally as they maintain the facade displayed on their social media. It seems like it's important to show their best selves to other people and appear independent and strong. However, being out of touch with their own emotions takes a toll, making the individual suffer even more.

In week 3, you will learn to identify your feelings correctly, track a particular emotion throughout the day, push through, and seek support when needed. You have emotions every day, even when you don't think about them, so prepare to learn to work with them.

I am in touch with my feelings and nurture those who elevate my being while taking care of myself.

CHECKING IN

Last week, you had many opportunities to practice working with values. Today, to review what you have already mastered, you'll take a few minutes to go outside of your home, perhaps to a park, if weather permits. Take some time to think about what you learned and accomplished. What values do you follow or display while being out? What is different today from what you do or feel on a typical day at home or work?

Keep in mind this is an opportunity to start creating the life you want to live. Use your senses to get in touch with nature. Look for vivid colors you like. Hear the sounds and try to recognize where they are coming from. Are there any pleasant smells? Is there an item you can touch while you are outside? How does it feel? How about taste? Are you eating or drinking something while you do this? How do you feel in general? When you are done or have to go back home, remind yourself that taking just three or five minutes a day to step out and enjoy the day is always beneficial to reduce depression and can also align you with your values.

Depression Doesn't Define You

People undoubtedly feel a range of emotions, positive and negative. When those emotions prevent you from doing your daily activities or affect your social interactions, it is necessary to kick the depression to the curb and keep going with the understanding that while the depression may be sitting close by, you are always in control. The main idea is not to let the negative feelings dominate, and to practice positive thinking, value setting, and emotional connectivity as often as possible.

Depression does not define you. When you're depressed, you may have a difficult time remembering what you were like before feeling depressed and struggle to separate the symptoms of depression from your regular self. However, depression is nothing more than a set of symptoms. You are much more than those symptoms; you have character, personality, strengths, and skills.

Most importantly, you will persist in life despite the illness. Next time you think about your depression, remind yourself about who you are. The symptoms may come to visit, but you are the one with the power to put them out to wait for a Lyft.

ACCEPTING THE NEGATIVE

People experience both positive and negative thinking. Individuals that experience depressive symptoms tend to deal more with negative thoughts while wishing they could be more positive. However, as human beings, it is perfectly fine and relatively normal to experience both types of thoughts. Negative thoughts are simply processes that our brain creates when not accustomed to reframing or thinking positively.

In therapy, there are different ways to deal with our thinking. One is the reframing process that comes from the cognitive behavioral model, changing all negative thinking into positive thoughts. For example: "I cannot find my keys. I am late, and I am going to get fired because this is the third time I've been late this week." Reframed thought: "I cannot find my keys, I am late, and I do not have to worry about getting fired because I will offer to make up the time during lunch or after work today or tomorrow." The other way a person can deal with negative thinking is acceptance. This concept is part of the acceptance and commitment therapy model. ACT involves accepting any negative thoughts and unwanted experiences outside of your control.

As you can see, it is essential to understand that negative emotions and thoughts will occur and affect all of us, so you must learn to accept and take these in stride. Unaccepted negative thoughts can cause unwanted emotions such as sadness, mood swings, anger, emptiness, hopelessness, worthlessness, self-blame, and guilt.

Quick Tip: Acceptance

THE SITUATION: At a family reunion, someone mentions something about you always looking sad and how they don't like that.

QUICK TIP: Take a deep breath. Then ask yourself the following questions: What made you feel what you are feeling? In what way did that person affect or hurt you? Do you still feel the same level of pain or sadness you did when you first heard it? Take a deep breath and look around the room for something that makes you feel good. Remind yourself that this is part of the acceptance process. Then go on with your day.

GETTING TO KNOW YOUR THOUGHTS

This activity will allow you to observe and enjoy your thoughts—not analyze them! This exercise will help you think before you respond and reflect on your answers after completing the activity.

Think about five words that describe you, such as student, professional, short, or tall. Write them down along with why you chose each word/adjective. When you are done, read the words you used to describe yourself. Then imagine that your inner self separates from your body, standing up next to you. Both of you read the words you wrote and your inner self, standing at a distance from you, tells you what they think. Do not force your thoughts to be negative or positive; just let the thinking process happen.

WORD/ADJECTIVE	INNER-SELF THOUGHTS
Ex: Quiet	Ex: You can be quiet or talkative; that does not define you as a person or make you more or less likable.

What are your thoughts about what your inner self shared?

BEING IN CONTROL OF YOUR THOUGHTS

You have been practicing different ways to recognize and control your thoughts. Doing this as a regular practice allows you to be in the present and to avoid living in the past or worrying about the future. This exercise helps you check your positivity level and reinforces what you have learned.

Read the following statements and circle the ones that apply to you. There are no right or wrong answers, nor do your answers have to fully represent your feelings; just go with what you feel the most.

A	B
I must know how to control my emotions to succeed in life.	*I do not need to control my emotions to succeed in life.*
Depression is bad.	*Depression is not good or bad. It is just a feeling.*
I am concerned about some of my reactions.	*I am not concerned about some of my reactions. They are typical, depending on the situation.*
It is necessary to eliminate negative thoughts as quickly as possible.	*Eliminating negative thoughts can cause issues. I can just let them be and accept them.*

KEY:

The majority of (a): difficulty accepting or working with your thoughts and letting your observing-self do its job.

The majority of (b): can accept or work with your thoughts, making it easier for your observing-self to do its job.

ACCEPTING REALITY

Values can be beneficial when you are working on accepting your own reality; they help you recognize something is not functional and give you an opportunity to find an acceptable reality and then plan. You may cherish certain values and try to live by them or have them in your life every day. Although it may not be easy to ensure other people live by their values, you can work to live by your own. This activity offers you an opportunity to use your values and practice reality acceptance.

In the following table, write down some realities about yourself that may be difficult to accept. Then write ideas reflecting acceptance and how you plan to accomplish them.

UNACCEPTABLE REALITY	ACCEPTABLE REALITY AND PLAN
Ex: I feel sad.	Ex: I feel sad, but I will make good use of my therapeutic tools, including my values and getting in touch with my emotions, by implementing body and emotional scans and practicing breathing techniques.

What can help you with accountability once you write your plans?

Coping Productively

Coping mechanisms, adaptive and maladaptive, are tactics or strategies you use to protect yourself and reduce unpleasant emotions during difficult times. Coping in relation to depressive emotions and feelings can include how you react when confronted with overwhelming or negative emotions. Coping can look like crying frequently, substance abuse, and isolation.

It's very common to see a person experiencing trauma shield themselves by using a coping mechanism. Challenging events, such as a separation, loss of employment, and the death of a loved one, can cause you to feel distressed. To adjust after any of these events, people use various behaviors, emotions, and thoughts, depending on the situation they are experiencing.

RESISTING THE NEGATIVE DEFAULT

As mentioned before, there are maladaptive or harmful coping habits. Perhaps you have heard of denial, withdrawal, bullying, and substance use. Here is a more detailed list of some other negative coping mechanisms we may not hear about as often:

Escape: *To cope with a difficulty, some individuals withdraw from family and friends and isolate themselves. They get lost in a solitary activity such as binge-watching Netflix or spending time viewing social media posts.*

Numbing: *This includes self-soothing behaviors. When people engage in these activities or behaviors, they are frequently aware of what they are getting into and specifically look for an activity that allows them to drown themselves in it. For example, they may try to quiet their pain by overeating, drinking too much, using drugs, or becoming workaholics.*

Risk-taking: *During difficult times or severe depression, some individuals look for an adrenaline rush through risk-taking behaviors such as speeding, unsafe sex, gambling, trying new drugs, and theft.*

Self-harm: *Some people engage in self-harming behaviors, such as cutting, sharing needles during drug use, and trying heavier drugs, to cope with harrowing situations.*

CHOOSING THE POSITIVE ALTERNATIVE

This is the other side of coping. These adaptive coping mechanisms provide people with a positive coping alternative, including pausing, acknowledging, and thinking. Other positive coping options are:

Support: *Talking about your emotions during and after a stressful event with a supportive and nonjudgmental person is beneficial.*

Breathing: *This allows you to oxygenate your brain and reduce negative emotions. Remember the 4-7-8 activity you learned earlier (page 27). That is an excellent example of an adaptive coping mechanism to use during difficult times.*

Relaxation: *This can include the body scanning you practiced earlier, as well as meditation, tai chi, mindfulness exercises, and the emotional freedom technique.*

Exercise: *Exercising can help you because it is a natural and healthy way to release stress. Yoga, walking, hiking, running, swimming, dancing, jumping, and any organized sport can be used here.*

Laughter: *Laughing during a problematic situation may help you maintain perspective and prevent the problem from becoming overwhelming. Try laughter yoga!*

No matter which one you choose, all adaptive coping mechanisms are helpful in their own way. Think of them as lifesavers while learning how to swim. You may need them only for some time, and then you will be ready to swim on your own.

Quick Tip: Coping with Depression

THE SITUATION: You have been feeling down and do not feel like going out. When someone invites you to an event or family gathering, you agree to go, but once the day comes, you self-isolate and avoid answering the phone or texts. Sometimes, if you really try, you message to let them know something came up and you will not be able to make it.

QUICK TIP: Prior to the day of the event, start reframing or using some of the mentioned coping mechanisms. That will improve your mood and increase your energy and the chemicals that fuel your brain.

MY COPING CONTRACT

People are complex creatures that live complicated lives. Because of that, they are not always capable of coping with the problems they face. That causes issues with depression and stress. To be able to handle any discomfort, it is recommended to use various coping methods like the ones we discussed.

After reviewing the coping mechanisms, you may have identified those that you think would be useful for you. Take a moment to go over the list again if you need to, then reflect on those you picked. Write them down and share why you find them useful or if you have used them before. Also, add how you think they may help you in the long run.

1.

2.

3.

4.

5.

Can you think of any other adaptive coping mechanisms that would work for you? List them here and add why you think they would work.

How does it make you feel knowing that positive coping mechanisms can help you to deal with depression and other problematic issues?

QUIZ TIME

Answer the following questions in your own words. Try not to go back through this chapter to look for the answers (you can go back after you finish the quiz if you need to). When you are done, review your answers.

1. What are coping mechanisms?

2. How do they help you cope with depressive symptoms?

3. If you had to choose only one coping mechanism, which one would it be?

4. Why that one?

5. Have you used any of the maladaptive mechanisms listed earlier?

6. Are you still using it/them?

7. Why?

8. Write a short summary of what you remember from the material covered this week, including the information you liked or found most helpful.

If you answered five to eight questions, congratulations! You are interested and have learned so much. If you answered one to four questions, you are trying, which says a lot about you. Go back and review if you need to, and concentrate on the implementation of ideas.

USING YOUR SENSES

Mindfulness activities, beneficial to cope with difficult situations, will not only be helpful to keep you in the present but also to allow your inner observer to grow. At the beginning of this chapter's activities, I mentioned that you will be using your creativity, imagination, and other mindfulness tools. The five senses will always be some of the best connectors to practice mindfulness. In this activity, you will revisit them but in a different format.

Complete the following lists and answer the questions.

1. List five things that you can envision:

2. What does your observing-self tell you about one, some, or all of them?

3. List four things that you can touch:

4. What does your observing-self tell you about one, some, or all of them?

5. List three sounds you hear:

6. What does your observing-self tell you about one, some, or all of them?

7. List two things you can smell where you are:

8. What does your observing-self tell you about one or both of them?

9. List one thing you can taste at this exact moment:

10. What does your observing-self tell you about it?

You did it! Great job collaborating with your observing-self!

PAUSE AND REFLECT

You are one step from finishing this week's activities. A sense of accomplishment is present. Equally satisfying will be using all the information you have learned here. As you prepare to finish this week, ask yourself the following questions and take a few minutes to go over your answers. You can write them down or just think about them. How interested are you in using or putting into practice the information you learned this week? How can you ensure that you stay in touch with your emotions? How interested are you in practicing body and emotional scanning to learn about how you feel on a regular basis? Most importantly, how can you continue taking care of yourself while practicing everything you have learned in this book so far?

I am very proud of you. You have completed another week, which tells me that you are willing to do what it takes to feel better. Depression may not disappear, but with the proper skills, you can minimize it to the point of making it almost nonexistent. Good job, and see you next week!

Key Takeaways

- This chapter guided you to learn to recognize and observe your thoughts.

- When you bury your emotions for a long time, it can be painful to face them later.

- You also learned that you need to become aware of sounds, smells, tastes, feelings, or thoughts to stop the negative thinking process.

- Mindfulness is one of the easiest ways to cope with difficult situations.

- Coping, in relationship to depressive emotions and feelings, can include how you react when confronted with overwhelming or negative emotions. Using your adaptive coping mechanisms can be very useful to fight depression.

WEEK 4

Getting Mentally Flexible

This week, you'll be learning about mental flexibility and how you think, positively or negatively. Cognitive flexibility is the process of adapting thinking patterns in order to respond to specific situations in less strict ways. This is an essential aspect of the healing process. Sometimes clients of mine hinder their own healing because the process of changing is uncomfortable, and it becomes challenging to adjust their thinking or accept new possibilities. It can be due to fear, because they have experienced difficult moments or situations, or because they don't know how to adjust their thoughts. In the following seven days, I'll provide you with tools that will help you embrace new ways of thinking, and you'll see it's not a challenging process if you set your mind and leave any concerns aside. Trust the method, and most of all, trust yourself. You've got this!

I open my mind to new ideas that can help me be better.

CHECKING IN

Last week, you completed the necessary work learning about your thoughts and emotions and how to work with them. You also became more familiar with how burying your thoughts and feelings can be uncomfortable and create more problems. Though it may be easier said than done, practicing at your own pace can facilitate the growth process. You do not have to talk to others about your thoughts all the time; you have other resources like journaling or using your senses to liberate yourself. Remember that positive, neutral, or negative thinking is a learned behavior that people start incorporating into their lives from an early age, adjusting it depending on their needs and experiences. The good news is that changing those behaviors is as simple as learning how.

Before you move to the next section, take a moment to reflect on your thoughts. Ask yourself if they have been primarily positive or negative, or a suitable combination of both, within the last week. Then think about how you respond to the negative thoughts: How does recognizing them change them? When you're done, continue with your reading or daily activities.

Understanding Thoughts

Your thoughts give you an opportunity to make decisions. They also offer a partial point of view that you develop or shape any way you want. They're an echo of the senses. For example, think of a dish that was very tasty. You can remember the smell, if it was hot, cold, salty, or sweet. Whatever made it tasty to you allowed you to bring the thoughts back today. By understanding how your thoughts work, you can control them in a positive way and ensure that you create healthy actions, too. By reframing and being present, you can understand how each thought shapes your behaviors.

IDENTIFYING THOUGHTS

To change your life and live with fewer depressive symptoms, it is necessary to change the way you think and, as a result, change your actions. To do so, you simply need to learn the skills and practice them. First, it is essential to recognize that you cannot control your thinking; thoughts and ideas come and go freely. For example, as you read this, try not to think of a stylish woman with a red beret strolling the streets of Paris while carrying a bouquet of flowers and a baguette in a market bag. You pictured that woman even knowing that you were not supposed to think about it! That is the way thoughts work. Your thought must already exist before it can be deemed positive or negative.

When you attempt to not think of something, your mind must think about it first. Thus, to suppress a thought, you have to replace that thought with something else or just accept the idea is there and move on. So, to identify your positive or negative thoughts, you can practice mindfulness, breathing exercises, meditation, tai chi, or emotional freedom technique, along with other known methods. By noticing your thoughts first, you will be able to take other beneficial steps to reduce depressive symptoms.

BUILDING YOURSELF UP

Negative self-talk is a result of negative thinking; it sabotages your healing process and your life in general. This type of self-talk can create depression, anxiety, and high-stress levels. This exercise is about identifying your patterns and determining if your self-talk is tearing you down or building you up.

Take a few minutes to think about a time when you experienced negative thoughts and your self-talk was destructive. Describe the situation and how you felt.

Here are six ways to manage negative self-talk:

1. Recognize that you're having unpleasant thoughts.

2. Reframe your negative thoughts into positive ones by challenging what you are telling yourself.

3. Ask yourself, *Is what I'm thinking helpful?*

4. Ask yourself, *Would I talk to a friend in the way I'm talking to myself.*

5. Control it by using the word "stop." For example, telling yourself, *I have to stop worrying about that.*

6. Accept that negative self-talk was wrong and moving on with your daily activities.

What can you start doing to better manage your negative self-talk? When and how can you start?

NEGATIVE THOUGHTS AND BELIEFS

Cognitive distortions are repetitive ways of thinking that are frequently inaccurate and negative. These negative thought patterns impact depression. You develop them as a way of coping with difficult situations, like when you are under a lot of stress or experiencing a traumatic event. Within the next exercise, you will practice and get more familiar with the concepts. You also will be able to add them to your tool kit and use them whenever you need to work with your thought recognition process. Some of the most common patterns are:

Self-blame. *Attributing the occurrence of an event or situation to oneself.*

Ex: It is my fault we missed the bus.

Black-and-white thinking. *Thinking in absolutes without a neutral option.*

Ex: I always ruin things.

Mind reading. *Making assumptions about what another person is thinking.*

Ex: They must be thinking I am not funny.

Crystal ball gazing. *Assuming that future events will turn out precisely as someone predicts them.*

Ex: They will be gone by the time we get there.

Overgeneralization. *Very common in people with depression. A way of thinking where people apply one experience to every present and future experience.*

Ex: I failed the test the first time, so I will never pass it.

Disqualifying the positive. *One of the most common negative thought patterns, and prevalent in people who experience depression. Rejecting all positive experiences as if they did not exist or count.*

Ex: Yes, but our team will never win again if we play against them.

Overactive thinking pattern. *Experiencing racing thoughts that overwhelm the person due to the constant repetition of the same cognitions.*

Ex: The exam is today, and I didn't study enough, so I'll not pass, fail the class, never graduate, and never find a job, so I'll be homeless.

Unrealistic expectations and thinking patterns. *Having a constant preoccupation with fantasies. It's also characterized by inner thoughts that lack connection with reality.*

Ex: They must find me very attractive. That's why they helped me.

Name-calling. *Using self-derogatory words to talk to themselves when something is not going the way they want. It's also known as negative self-talking.*

Ex: I am a drunk.

Catastrophizing. *Expecting disaster to strike no matter what.*

Ex: I will lose my job because of my fear of public speaking.

Ruminating. *Analyzing concerns or repetitively worrying without doing anything to create a positive change.*

Ex: I shouldn't have said that to them. What was I thinking? Why did I say that?

Quick Tip: Deleting Your Thinking Errors

THE SITUATION: You keep having negative thoughts but do not know what to do with them.

QUICK TIP: Everyone makes thinking mistakes, but those mistakes become problematic when negative thoughts become chronic. It can then become challenging to disengage from that way of thinking. When you learn to recognize negative thinking, you make it easier to think more positively and feel better about yourself. So, remember to stop every day to scan and review your thoughts and emotions. That is practicing mindfulness. Determine how you see yourself, others, and the world around you.

A PENNY FOR YOUR THOUGHTS

Negative thoughts and beliefs can affect your behavior without you realizing it. That is why it is important to become aware of your thoughts and replace them with more rational ones or accept them. Becoming familiar with them and practicing how to identify them will help you learn and practice future activities.

The following table shows six types of thoughts. Review them and write down an example for each of the different types.

THOUGHT TYPE	GIVEN EXAMPLE	MY EXAMPLE
Black-and-white thinking	They either love me or hate me.	
Assumption thinking (crystal ball gazing; mind reading)	They haven't called me. I didn't get the job.	
Catastrophizing thinking	There is no good food in this city because this one restaurant was not good.	
Self-blame thinking	I must be the reason why the team always loses.	
Zero-positive thinking (disqualifying the positive)	They're just inviting me because they need me.	
Positive thinking (reframing)	I can't find my keys, and I'll get late to work, then fired for being tardy again. *Reframe:* Maybe I was going to have an accident if I left earlier, so it is good I will be driving a few minutes later.	

THOUGHTS, EMOTIONS, AND BEHAVIORS

When you take some time to step back and see if there are ideas or behaviors that you need to let go of, you continue to practice thought-challenging and acceptance. This is an excellent way to keep training your brain to combat negative thoughts. This activity will help you recognize and accept what needs to stay and what needs to go.

Create a list of five thoughts you would like to let go of. Go over your responses to familiarize yourself with them when you are done.

THOUGHTS THAT I WOULD LIKE TO RELEASE	EMOTIONS THAT I WOULD LIKE TO RELEASE	BEHAVIORS THAT I WOULD LIKE TO RELEASE
Ex: My friends do not like to go out with me.	Ex: Disappointment	Ex: Agreeing to go out but cancel last minute

Do you see any patterns?

How do you feel about what you see?

What changes can you implement to let go?

Breaking Negative Thought Patterns

Breaking negative thought patterns is all about using the right the tools and practicing new skills. Accepting that thoughts are just that—thoughts—and nothing more can accelerate the healing process. Remember, when you hold on to your negative thoughts, making them more entrenched, you have difficulty letting go. They become your reality, creating anxiety or more depressive symptoms. To break the pattern, you must step back, observe your thoughts without getting lost in them, and acknowledge them to then let them go. Throughout this book, you'll have opportunities to practice these skills in a safe space so that you can confidently use the skills in your everyday life.

IDENTIFYING TRIGGERS

Triggers can be situations, places, events, smells, or people that set off a flashback or take a person back to the moment and place where something traumatic was experienced. This can make the individual relive the pain or feel sadness, anxiety, fear, or depression. The emotional reaction created by the disturbing memory can range from mild to severe, depending on the person and how much the experience affected them. When triggered, your reactions can be unexpected, causing you to feel out of control. You can be better prepared when you're aware of your triggers and learn how to respond, ultimately enhancing your ability to cope and avoid severe symptoms.

Identifying your triggers is not complicated, but it does take practice. You can start by thinking about things that create negative thoughts or reactions. Some common triggers may include dates when you lost a loved one, watching the news, family conflicts, a person that harmed you, lack of communication with a loved one, illness, seeing people arguing, people yelling, a dark room, being alone, specific smells, and so on.

You can also observe the physical and emotional reactions you have when you encounter specific situations or people. The physical symptoms may include nausea, shaking, crying, rapid heartbeat, dizziness, stuttering, sweating, and chest pain. Emotionally, you can experience fear, anxiety, sadness, or panic attacks.

You can also identify your response to a specific stimulus, retracing your steps to learn where the response comes from, and repeating the process if you can't identify the trigger the first time.

Understanding why something is particularly triggering is helpful because it allows you to be prepared and eventually diminish the symptoms caused by the trigger.

DISCOVERING YOUR TRIGGERS

Triggers can present in many ways, shapes, and forms. They can be places, people, and even smells. When you take the time to recognize what affects you or triggers you, it becomes easier to avoid experiencing the negative emotions they create; it becomes automatic.

Read the following questions and then answer in detail. After you are done, review your answers and take a mental picture of what you wrote. Allow yourself to feel the emotions you experience while reading what you wrote instead of avoiding them.

What situations, people, activities, or places do you tend to avoid?

What have you withdrawn from, dropped out of, or quit?

When/where do you procrastinate?

You have identified some triggers. This will be helpful as you move on and continue practicing how to work with negative emotions.

WHAT IS YOUR PERCEPTION?

This activity is another tool to help you understand your thoughts. It will help you practice identifying your thoughts and eventually create the habits of positive self-talk and acceptance.

Draw a horizontal line in the middle of the circle. The upper semicircle will be used to write down all the negative words or ideas that arise while thinking of yourself, as well as what others have used to describe you. After you are done with the negatives, go to the bottom half of the circle and write down all positive words or phrases that you can think of. This can include any positive comments you've used toward yourself and those others have used to describe you. Remember to write down the words as they come to you without taking too long to think about them.

When you are done, take a few minutes to reflect on how you felt while writing. What was easier to recall: the positive or the negative? Did something trigger you? Notice all the feelings you have experienced while completing this activity. What do they tell you about the need to change something in your life?

REFRAMING REACTIONS

Reframing is one of the most used techniques by therapists who practice cognitive behavioral therapy (CBT). This practice helps clients identify automatic negative thoughts and replace them with more positive ones. You can use various strategies to manage reactions to negative thoughts and triggers, such as challenging your thoughts.

Challenging your thoughts is about questioning them and evaluating if they are facts or just negative cognitions. You can do that by looking for facts before assuming the negative is true. *What evidence do I have to believe that is true?* I often ask before jumping to conclusions. When you can challenge your thoughts, then you can also move away from the negative by looking for a more positive side. For example, you might decide, *If I do not have any evidence, I should not worry about it.*

Cognitive defusion is the technique used by therapists who practice acceptance and commitment therapy. It involves learning how to separate from your thoughts by taking a step back and being an observer. Instead of getting lost in your thoughts, you let them come and go away as if they were just clouds floating in the sky. You observe your thinking, initiating the ACT process. You see the thoughts for what they are, nothing more or less than reflections of your depression. This allows you to reframe and understand that the depression is visiting but never staying forever.

There is no right or wrong when it comes to reframing reactions. You can use what works better for you when it feels right. What matters the most when using reframing is that you keep practicing it. Think of it as going to the gym. The more you go, the better the results. The same happens when you reframe, defuse, or challenge your thoughts.

Quick Tip: Be Aware of Your Triggers

THE SITUATION: You are in a dark room and need to go get an item from another room. You cannot turn any lights on, and you need the item now. As you start thinking about how dark it is, you start feeling worried, dizzy, nauseous, and overwhelmed. Negative thoughts start invading you, making you feel more concerned by the minute.

QUICK TIP: Stop, take a deep breath, and use your senses to notice what is around you. Recite the alphabet or count until you feel better. These two activities are grounding techniques that help you relax, stay calm, and think clearer.

RECOGNIZING TRIGGERS IN YOUR LIFE

Almost anything can be a trigger. Recognizing what, when, or where creates negative emotions in you is essential. For each of the following categories, list at least three examples of things that trigger you. You don't have to fill in every line, but take your time to remember and identify as many triggers as you can.

PEOPLE	*Ex: A family member*
THINGS	*Ex: The jeans you wore on a specific day*
SITUATIONS	*Ex: Driving at night*

CONTINUED ▶

EVENTS	*Ex: A work meeting*
PLACES	*Ex: An elevator or other closed space*
THOUGHTS	*Ex: A traumatic memory such as a car accident*

When you are done, describe in detail your biggest triggers, including what they are and how you feel when you think about them or experience them. If possible, add what caused each one to become a trigger.

If you need some help to find ways to work with those triggers, go back to the reframing reactions section and pick the best ways to deal with the negative thoughts and triggers.

What will you do to reduce the effects caused by these triggers?

PAUSE AND REFLECT

You have learned and accomplished so much this week. You started with mental flexibility and moved on to recognizing negative and positive thoughts as well as triggers and how to deal with them. Before you complete this last activity, take a moment to reflect on this week. Think about what held your attention the most, as well as any challenging material. There is no right or wrong, just what you think.

When you are done, use the following space to write a letter to yourself congratulating you for everything you have done this week. Include information about what you covered and learned. You can define some of the terms or explain them in your own words. Also, share how learning this material will help you and how you plan to incorporate it into your life. Working with what triggers you can make writing this letter somewhat challenging. If that happens, remind yourself that only you will read it, and there is no right or wrong. This is your letter, and you have three vital tools to deal with negative thinking: reframing, defusion, and challenging your thoughts.

Key Takeaways

- Everyone has negative thoughts. What varies is how each person manages them.

- Breaking negative thought patterns is about practicing the therapeutic skills you are learning. Accepting that thoughts are just that and nothing more can accelerate your healing.

- When an intrusive thought is taking over and you recognize it, be intentional and stop the thought by replacing it with a happy one.

- A trigger is a stimulus that reminds you of a traumatic event. Knowing how to identify it and what to do with it can help you reduce the negative symptoms.

- Be patient with yourself.

Handling Stress and Anxiety

High five! You have completed another chapter and are now on your way to tackling two critical roadblocks that are closely related to depression: stress and anxiety. Although there is no clear answer about the relationship between the three, we know that depression and anxiety typically go hand in hand, and stress is an extra factor that exacerbates the symptoms of both. This week, you will be learning more about how they interact, the cycle they create, and how to break this cycle by practicing specific skills and creating a personal tool kit to help you through this journey. As you learn this week, the most crucial part is to continue with these practices every day and as often as you can. The more intentional you are, the easier it will be for you to implement positive changes.

I take care of myself and don't let stress or anxiety control my life. I am in control.

CHECKING IN

Last week, you worked with negative thoughts and identifying your triggers. This is another opportunity to refresh what you learned by completing a quick activity.

Find a place at home, the office, or anywhere you can be alone. Make sure you take your workbook with you, so you can answer the questions that follow the mindfulness practice. Sit down in a comfortable place. It can be a chair, couch, or bed. You can even sit on the floor as long as you're comfy. Set a timer for five minutes.

- Close your eyes and let your thoughts come and go as if they were clouds pushed by the wind. Some will be positive, and others will be negative. You may start hearing your inner critic making negative comments.

- Don't overthink; just be aware of what goes through your mind. If you feel like responding to the inner critic, remember that its voice and thoughts are the clouds that disappear with the wind.

When the timer rings, answer these questions:

1. What was one of the negative thoughts you had?

2. On a scale of 0 to 5, how easy was it to observe the thoughts and let them go?

The Stress and Depression Loop

Stress can cause negative thoughts, and negative thoughts can cause stress. They are mutually reinforcing and can worsen each other. Making some changes to your lifestyle can help you break this cycle. That starts with a positive mindset, implementing a healthy diet, making time for you, removing known stressors, and being patient. Most importantly, you must keep an open attitude, practice acceptance, and avoid thinking that nothing you do will make a difference. It will if you work on it.

WHAT IS STRESS?

When you think about stress, maybe something negative comes to mind. However, stress can be positive, such as the jitters that accompany getting ready to accept an award. Stress creates feelings that can help or hinder your daily functioning. Stress can make you feel overwhelmed and incapable of coping with any type of pressure, or it can help you accomplish a task at the last minute. Some of its more common symptoms are nervousness, inability to focus, restlessness, agitation, rapid heart rate, lack of sleep, nausea, irritability, and increase of energy. When you are stressed out, it is common to feel over-energized (positive stress) or have restless nights, feel tired, and still need to keep working or taking care of responsibilities at home (negative stress). As that tension escalates, you feel more frustrated and anxious.

Anxiety is often connected to stress and depression. The simplest definition of anxiety is a feeling of extreme worry that affects people dealing with known or unknown unwanted circumstances. Anxiety can be described as a feeling of fear about an impending event with an uncertain outcome. As a therapist, I can share that it can be a debilitating emotion. It keeps the sufferer living in the unforeseeable future, constantly worrying about something that has not yet happened and maybe never will. Anxiety symptoms can include nausea, palpitations, difficulty breathing, lightheadedness, a fainting-like sensation, sweaty palms, and stomachaches.

The relationship between stress and anxiety is close. Not reducing one or both may affect your mental, physical, and emotional health, preventing you from living your vision and purpose. Not working on them may also create feelings of irritability or anger, preventing you from enjoying happy moments. To live a more balanced life, it is beneficial to work on letting go of both. The following activities will allow you to learn and practice that.

IDENTIFYING YOUR STRESSORS

Stress have various causes. I describe most stressors as threats to yourself, coming out of nowhere, new to you, and making you lose your sense of control. Think of a boss or a formidable family member that calls you out of nowhere, stating that you need to talk, and you do not have the option of saying no. The first thing that comes to your mind might be *What did I do? What do they need to talk about?* An unknown future becomes a cause of stress.

Take a few minutes to go over this list and mark stressors you have experienced within the last six months. When you are done, answer the questions at the end.

☐ Loss of employment   ☐ Financial difficulties

☐ Breakup   ☐ Crime

☐ Severe illness   ☐ Meeting a work deadline

☐ Separation from a loved one   ☐ Missing a flight

☐ Moving   ☐ Dental surgery

☐ Change of employment   ☐ Divorce

☐ Marriage   ☐ Severe loneliness

☐ Family violence   ☐ Drug abuse (self or loved one)

Have any of those stressors affected your depression? In what way?

Did the stress last indefinitely? How did you end it?

THE IMPACT OF STRESS ON DEPRESSION

The word "stress" has been misused, and some people no longer pay attention to it. It's common to hear someone say, *I am so stressed out* or *It was a stressful day*, making stress sound normal. Normalizing it has made it lose its impact, inviting people to ignore it when it really affects them. The real meaning of stress is a severe state of emotional or mental strain.

Actual stress can be positive but also so detrimental that it negatively affects depression management, disrupting positive habits and strategies. It also affects the individual's routine or daily activities. The interruption of the healthy routine can lead to a relapse of old thought patterns and harmful coping methods, furthering depression. Hence the importance of recognizing stress symptoms and mitigating them to break the cycle.

Although there are many examples of how stress impacts depression, I've selected the following two examples to give you a clearer idea. First, stress affects relationships: When you're stressed out, you can feel irritated, withdrawn, quiet, or argumentative. Without trying to create problems, you can respond poorly and hurt someone's feelings or initiate an argument. If you have suffered from depression in the past and are now under stress, people around you may say they have to walk on eggshells. That makes communication and interactions complex for all, disrupting structure and routines. Second, stress affects responsibilities. Sometimes it's difficult to leave the bed or take a bath—and even more difficult to go to work or complete a project. Keeping consistent routines and having structure can help prevent stress from damaging your relationships and responsibilities.

Quick Tip: Maintaining Structure and Routine

THE SITUATION: You wake up feeling more depressed this morning than yesterday. Having to be at work in an hour, you cover your face with the blanket. Then you remember that a project is due this afternoon, adding to the high level of stress you already had. You have to get ready, but you just can't.

QUICK TIP: Uncover your face, take a deep breath while counting to four, hold your breath while counting to seven, then exhale while counting to eight. Repeat this exercise three times. When you are done, think of a way to reward yourself today for getting up and sticking to your routine.

PRACTICING BEING IN THE PRESENT

Living in the here and now is not simply an aphorism. It is a style of life recommended to people who are struggling with depression or stress. The following activity is very popular when practicing being in the present. It is an excellent way to reconnect with yourself, too; paying attention to your surroundings is a perfect way to be present.

Sit down in a comfortable place wherever you are now, indoors or outdoors. Complete these sentences using what you encounter around you.

Ex: I recognize something green—I see trees, the grass, a vase, my curtains, etc.

I hear something close or far away:

I feel something soft:

I recognize something big:

I hear something nice:

I feel something smooth:

I recognize something red:

My favorite thing that I saw, felt, or heard was

because

BECOMING A "JOURNALIST"

This exercise can help you set the right tone for releasing stress every day. It prepares you to start journaling, which allows you to check in with your emotions regularly, track moods, and let out anxieties that can't be voiced. Today, you will use the given prompt, but in the future, you can come up with your own or just write whatever you are thinking or feeling.

This activity can be completed at any time of the day, perhaps before you get out of bed, during a break while relaxing in the afternoon, or before you go to sleep. There is no right or wrong, so just let your mind dictate whatever it wants to share, and write as you think. Remember that you want to stay focused on the present. So, if you start thinking about the past too much or worrying about things that you have to do in the future, regroup your thoughts and come back to what you are feeling or thinking in the here and now.

Using the following prompts, take a few minutes to write down what you think.

Today, I am taking the time to write and share how I feel or think. The first idea that came to my mind about this moment is that today . . .

Read what you wrote. How do you feel after letting go through journaling? What was positive about writing?

Breaking the Cycle

When you overthink about the future, you deal with negative thoughts. This overthinking can be detrimental to your health. The more you overthink and stress, the less clarity of mind and time you have. Managing stress levels is not complicated; you just need to have the right tools and be intentional enough to use them every day. You will learn more about them in the following sections.

Learning to manage your stress is beneficial to stabilize your blood pressure and glucose levels, decrease anxiety and depressive symptoms, improve your relationships, and have better days. To break this cycle, you have to change how you approach your personal and professional life. You can do this by putting yourself under less pressure to perform; sharing responsibilities or delegating; taking on fewer duties at home, school, or work; and removing yourself from stressful situations and relationships that harm your well-being.

BODY SYNC

Some therapists use a holistic approach to treat depression. A holistic approach involves working with the body, mind, and spirit. This approach helps people because it addresses the leading cause of the problems, not just the symptoms.

This is a short compilation of practices that include relaxation techniques to manage stress and anxiety:

Yoga: *A group of mental, spiritual, and physical practices that aim to control and still the mind through postures and meditations. There are many schools of yoga, encompassing both modern and traditional practices, and one of its uses is mindfulness. Yoga originated in ancient India.*

Meditation: *A practice where a person focuses the mind on a thought or particular idea to achieve calmness or a specific mental state. It can be free or guided.*

Mindfulness: *A stress-reduction practice that allows people to free their minds from negativity or release stress by focusing on being intentionally aware of their feelings in the moment.*

Deep breathing: *This is one of the most used ways to reduce stress. It consists of breathing through your nose and exhaling through your mouth.*

Tai chi: *This is a martial art practiced to reduce stress and as self-defense with several health benefits, such as vital signs regulation. Tai chi is often practiced in groups at public parks or other open spaces.*

Emotional freedom technique (EFT): *A form of stress reduction that focuses on tapping specific body points with your fingers.*

All of these can be practiced individually or in a group. There are videos online where you can watch people practicing them (see Resources, page 175).

PRACTICING MINDFULNESS

Mindfulness activities are popular for a reason: they work. When you complete this exercise, keep in mind it has a specific purpose: to be mindful. This exercise also invites you to learn more about your emotions and accept them as they are. Before writing your answers, repeat the following: *I am here now, and as I notice my thoughts and feelings, I accept the way I feel.*

Today, I am

and I accept how I feel because

Being in the here and now, to me, means that I

I accept that I have different feelings depending on my situation and today I chose

to feel

because it benefits me by

As my mind creates some thoughts while I complete this activity, I allow myself to

those thoughts and keep what benefits me. Everything else, I

and do not bring it back into my life.

I end this activity reminding myself that I am in control and can do the following to

improve my life:

Repeat again: *I am here now, and as I notice my thoughts and emotions, I accept the way I feel.*

BEING IN THE HERE AND NOW

One of the primary purposes of being mindful is to reduce stress and depressive symptoms in order to live a good and healthy life. This exercise is about observing your thoughts in the present. Read the following prompts and then add any thoughts that cross your mind without assigning any judgments. When you are done, read your responses and reflect on them to practice mindfulness.

When I cultivate unselfconsciousness, I stop worrying about how I act, and others judging me also becomes unimportant.

Thoughts:

When I stop worrying about the future and allow myself to fully experience the present, I am genuinely savoring life.

Thoughts:

Practicing deep breathing is essential. I allow myself to practice mindfulness, helping myself feel calm when I do that. I also improve my communications and relationships with others since I feel more relaxed.

Thoughts:

When I purposely lose track of time, I have more opportunities to enjoy the present.

Thoughts:

When I take the time to see how I feel and acknowledge that I am experiencing emotions, I improve my ability to accept, heal, and deal with my depression.

Thoughts:

I can be more mindful by noticing what is around me and improving my mindfulness. I can do this at home or in a public place.

Thoughts:

WELLNESS TOOL KIT

A wellness tool kit is an excellent way to be proactive about caring for yourself when you will need it most. This tool kit provides you with the essential information, ideas, skills, resources, and fun practices that can help you deal with depression symptoms, stress, and unwanted negative moods. It can contain activities such as mindfulness, meditation, and breathing exercises. Each tool kit is unique since everyone responds differently to stressful situations or life events. You get to create your own kit, including the best tools to maintain a healthy emotional state.

Your wellness tool kit can include:

- **Hobbies:** Playing sports, playing cards, watching movies, hiking, going for a walk in the park, baking, fixing cars, traveling. Add your favorite hobby or activity here, too!

- **Self-care activities:** Lighting a scented candle, eating healthy, taking a nap, journaling, meditation, sleeping, yoga, practicing tai chi, being mindful, talking to friends, taking a bath, practicing breathing exercises, talking to a therapist, attending a support group, practicing creative visualization.

- **Social activities:** Visiting or calling a friend, attending a party, joining an interest group, traveling with a group, volunteering in the community.

- **Learning activities:** Taking an art or music class, going back to school, enrolling in an online course, learning a skill.

You can get other ideas for your tool kit by paying attention to what you do that makes you happy or calm.

Quick Tip: Changing Patterns

THE SITUATION: You've been feeling down. This isn't the first time you've felt like canceling tonight's outing with your friends. If you're not proactive, the depressive symptoms will increase, making it challenging for you to shake them off. You wish you felt well enough to go tonight.

QUICK TIP: Don't call your friends yet. Without thinking about the plan, wander for a few minutes around your home, turn on the music, and take a bath. Pick a nice outfit and spray yourself with your favorite cologne or perfume. Take five deep breaths and visualize how tonight would be perfect. How do you feel about going now?

MY HAPPY PLACE

The power of the mind is infinite. According to Dr. David R. Hamilton, your brain does not distinguish between whether you are facing a stressful situation or imagining it. In the same way, when you imagine being on vacation and visualize a beautiful place for a few minutes, the brain does not recognize the difference between imagining it and being there for real. The benefits are the same. Today, you will take a mindful imaginary walk through your happy place. This can be the beach, the mountains, or any location that brings you happiness when you think about it.

1. Start by thinking about a place you enjoy spending time at—somewhere that nourishes and recharges you. Then take a few minutes to situate yourself in a comfortable place.

2. Close your eyes and imagine yourself arriving at your happy place.

3. Use your senses to explore what you can recognize, smell, hear, taste, and touch. Spend some time enjoying what you have there.

4. When you are done, imagine yourself coming back to where you are sitting now.

5. Write down what you experienced, including what you saw, smelled, touched, tasted, and heard. Be as detailed as possible.

How do you feel after visiting your happy place?

PAUSE AND REFLECT

It has been another great week for you since you completed another section of your workbook! I am proud of you. You continue learning so much. As you prepare to finish this week, ask yourself the following questions and take a few minutes to go over your answers. (You can write them down or just think about them.) *How do I plan to continue practicing mindfulness using my surroundings or imagination every day? When I worry about the future too much, how will I bring myself back to the present as soon as possible? What practices will I use to continue being in touch with the present? What will I do to avoid dwelling in the past?*

I believe you are ready for another great week. You have completed this week, and that tells me that you are willing to keep going and do what it takes to feel even better. Remember that with the proper skills, but mostly with practice, you can minimize your depression to the point of making it almost nonexistent. You are doing a wonderful job. See you next week!

Key Takeaways

- Stress can be a positive or negative emotion that creates feelings that can help or harm your daily functioning.

- Using your wellness tool kit is a great way to reduce depressive symptoms.

- Being mindful, or living in the present, does not require you to ignore your past or future. You can still think about those times without forgetting that what truly matters is enjoying your present experiences.

- The more mindful you are, the more you live in a positive reality.

- When you live in the present, you can be more grateful, which benefits you and others around you.

WEEK 6

The Positive You

From a positive point of view, you're almost done with your workbook. You have learned, practiced, and reflected on values. You have come to terms with your emotions. You have become more mentally flexible. And you better understand how to handle stress and anxiety as they interrelate to depression.

This week, you will continue practicing what you have learned, and you will cover positivity. The "positive you" is your natural self. That *you* gets overshadowed by depression sometimes, preventing you from enjoying activities or feeling as happy as you want. As you complete the material, you'll embrace the positive, review your strengths and hopes, and create a helpful positivity routine. Remember, you continue to be in control—but you're healthier, stronger, and much better than when you got on board this incredible discovery ride!

I have a bright and cheerful light within that energizes me and makes me feel good all day long.

CHECKING IN

Last week, you worked on reducing stress, anxiety, and depression through mindfulness and creating a tool kit. This is a quick review of last week's material.

Answer the following using true or false. Then check your results.

	True	False
1. I prefer not thinking too much about the past.		
2. I don't have to have a plan for the week.		
3. In transit, I like to look at people, streets, or signs.		
4. I pay attention to my surroundings and remember things I recognize.		
5. It's easy for me to remember names or faces.		
6. I enjoy taking time to look at the stars.		
7. When I go shopping, I enjoy looking around.		
8. When I go to a restaurant, I don't rush.		
9. I spend most of my time doing something fun or productive instead of binge-watching a show.		

If your answers were mostly true, you live in the present and will enjoy working on the following exercises. If your answers were primarily false, this chapter is going to be a great resource and you will benefit from the exercises, so continue working on the following activities.

Embracing the Positive

Positivity is about seeing the good side of things and being optimistic the majority of the time. Even when you do not believe it, you can come up with a better reason why something happened. Positive thinking is beneficial for your health because it lowers stress and regulates your vital signs. Practicing positivity when you feel depressed or sick improves your general well-being. When you are sick, your body recuperates faster. When you feel down, you attain emotional balance, which helps your brain function appropriately.

Embracing the positive is an excellent opportunity to change your life for the best, since it:

- Increases your life span.

- Regulates your cardiovascular health.

- Lowers the levels of negative stress.

- Increases your mental resilience.

- Helps you be more productive.

- Improves relationships and communication.

- Enhances gratitude feelings.

YOUR STRENGTHS AND HOPES

Everyone has strengths, even when they're hard to pinpoint. The question is not if you have them but if you can identify them and understand their importance as opportunities for growth. Similarly, we all have hopes, but we sometimes forget about them if a dark cloud is following us. Hopes are interests and motivators, and they are fueled by strengths. Imagine, for example, that you want to finish a project. You will need to make use of your strengths, like tenacity, commitment, and trustworthiness, to do it. If none of those are present, the hopes and goals are not impossible, but it will take you much longer to realize them. Hence, to see something come to fruition, you need to know your strengths and use them to your advantage.

Having hope shows that you believe in the future and in better outcomes in your life. As you can imagine, hope is firmly linked to positive thinking. Just like positive people, hopeful people are less affected by depression. When I ask clients about what they are hopeful about or what their strengths are, and they say "nothing" and "none," I can immediately tell they are experiencing depressive symptoms. The silver lining is that people can learn to find hope and identify their strengths—and then use them both. If you concentrate on channeling hope in a proactive manner, you will start believing that good things do happen, and your strengths start becoming more visible to you and others.

Quick Tip: Kick Doubt to the Curb

THE SITUATION: You have not finished a project, and you see it waiting for you for the tenth time. As you get closer to the deadline, you start doubting yourself, telling yourself that you don't have the strength to do it. You doubt you can finish, so you begin losing all hope to meet the deadline.

QUICK TIP: Take a few deep breaths and mentally go over your strengths list. Pick the top three that stand out from that list. How can you incorporate those strengths to help you finish the project? How will you reward yourself when done? You have what it takes to complete it!

YOUR STRENGTHS

People who know, accept, and frequently use their strengths tend to be happier and may find it easier to achieve their goals. This exercise will help you get a clear idea of your strengths and how you can use them to your benefit. Some positive attributes or strengths will be easy for you to pick right away. Others may come after a moment of reflection, so take your time to complete the activity.

Identify your strengths from this list and circle them. You can add some, if not all of yours are listed here:

Wisdom   Empathy   Friendliness   Artistic skills

Trustworthiness   Love   Care   Curiosity   Honesty

Perseverance   Persistence   Interest   Kindness   Creativity

Enthusiasm   Involvement   Leadership   Courage

Understanding   Fairness   Patience   Tactfulness   Forgiveness

High self-esteem   Self-control   Thankfulness

Sense of humor   Desire   Respect   Sportsmanship

Discipline   Commitment   Independence   Hope   Confidence

Positivity   Cheerfulness   Confidence

1. What are your thoughts after reviewing your strengths?

2. How do your strengths define you as a person?

_____

_____

_____

_____

_____

FINDING THE SILVER LINING

The silver lining of something encompasses the good aspects of any problematic situation. It doesn't matter how challenging the problem is; you most likely can find a positive way to see it. When you notice that silver lining, you have an optimistic view that helps you stay afloat during challenging times.

In acceptance and commitment therapy, focusing on that positive side without ignoring the negative is essential. We call this cognitive defusion. Remember that defusion aims not to prevent negative thoughts but to acknowledge them and help you reduce the influence of these unwanted or negative thoughts on your behavior. In other words, you work through the difficulties by looking at the opportunities and accepting the negative aspects.

Defusion is a very effective technique in helping people cope with negative feelings. It is recommended to individuals that suffer from depression as well as anxiety. It invites people to create space between themselves and their negative thoughts. An easy activity to understand how it works is placing your hands about two inches in front of your face. You will see only your hands. Now move them away, creating some space by extending your arms. Your view is broader, and you see your hands and other things in the area. In the same way, defusion helps you start seeing your thoughts: After identifying any negative ones, you can move away from them, see more positive views, and think more optimistically.

DEFUSION 101

Writing or journaling allows you to unpack specific things that bother you. A good way to practice cognitive defusion is by thanking the mind. When you do that, you show that you are not taking it too seriously. In other words, you are being sarcastic or purposely laughing at the mind to de-escalate your thinking. Changing your relationship with your negative thoughts by not taking them too seriously and giving positivity a chance to take over helps alleviate depressive symptoms.

In this activity, you will write five entries thanking your mind for five negative thoughts you recently had. For example, you can say something like:

"My friends went to eat together and did not invite me. As I remembered the incident and thought about it, I felt angry. However, I thanked my mind for creating all the thoughts that came after that. My mind helped me realize that I was assuming what happened without knowing if it was real. I was making something bigger than what it was. Thanks for the feedback, mind!"

1.

2.

3.

4.

5.

MY POSITIVITY, GOALS, AND HOPES CONTRACT

Practicing positivity also involves creativity. This activity is all about being creative and having fun. Take your time. The most important part is that you enjoy yourself while learning and coming up with the perfect answers for you.

List some daily positive thoughts, goals, and affirmations on the following lines. This helps you practice positivity and set goals. You do not have to use all of them every day. One or a few a day will work just fine. I am providing some examples that you can use, but strive to create your own to make them more personal.

- **Positive affirmations examples:** I am enough. This week, I chose to be confident.

- **Positive thoughts examples:** It will be better next time. Everything is a learning experience.

- **Positive goals examples:** I will finish the project on time. I will create a positive routine to follow this month.

1.

2.

3.

4.

5.

6.

7.

8.

9.

10.

Now that I am done, I accept this as a binding contract where I promise to practice or incorporate at least one every day and come up with new ones as needed.

Signature: Date:

Create a Positivity Routine

A positivity routine is a highly recommended tool for your tool kit. It includes a series of ideas or activities that you can do at a particular time or day: a regular practice in a fixed order. What you do during that set time is entirely up to you, as long as it's positive, beneficial, and increases your well-being, self-esteem, and hope. The main goal of a routine is to have a foundation of practices that you can count on and build the rest from there. You will create your positivity routine soon.

BENEFITS OF ROUTINE

Some days, people who experience depression can find it very difficult to get out of bed, feed themselves, or complete any daily activity. Following a daily routine can be highly beneficial. It decreases the negative emotions that come from not fulfilling responsibilities and feeling like a failure day after day. Patients with depression often tell me that the inability to care for themselves makes them feel like they are falling. Even worse, the lower they fall, the harder it becomes to get up.

This downward spiral is difficult to get out of, mainly because depression is lying to you, making you feel that you are unloved, alone, or unwanted when you fall. In these cases, you need to create a positive routine that can help you feel better to be able to accomplish more. Creating and following an easy and reliable routine can improve mental health by decreasing depressive symptoms. As a result, you will be more likely to complete more of your daily activities. Yes, it is a cycle! When you commit to a daily routine, specific practices will get you out of bed and ready to start your day. You need to start by designing a routine and then sticking to it. And if the practices you include in your routine are proven to reduce symptoms of depression, even better!

ARE YOU READY FOR THIS?

Creating your own positivity routine is all about combining knowledge and creativity to come up with your own piece of art. This activity will walk you through the process. Follow the prompts, and then revise what you wrote when you are done.

Write a list: *Include everything you need to do daily. This is not a to-do list but a list of ideas. If it helps, write throughout the day, instead of in one sitting.* Ex: Take a shower, eat, check emails, etc.	
Your structured day: *Think about when you have the most energy or work best and list important activities around that time. 5–11 a.m.: List all your early activities and the most difficult ones.* Ex: Go to the gym, clean the bathroom, etc. *12–5 p.m.: List the least enjoyable activities and use time wisely if your energy level is higher.* Ex: Make phone calls, run errands, etc. *6–10 p.m.: List all preparation and organization activities.* Ex: Pack lunch, get clothes ready, etc.	
Be specific: *Break down each day by time and be as detailed as possible.* Ex: 5–8 a.m. Self-care; 9–10 a.m. Emails and work or house projects; 11 a.m.–12 p.m. Clean a room or have a meeting.	
Be flexible: *You may need to go to the doctor or host a friend, so be flexible because sometimes you will have to change your plans. Write down what you can do when the unexpected happens.*	
Test it: *Try your routine for fifteen days. Keep track of how things are working out and how you feel. Nothing is set in stone, so you can always change something. You can write your change here, too. Remember, this is your masterpiece!*	

FINDING YOUR ROUTINE

Good routines can be so varied, interesting, and fun. That's because you create your own. I will offer some ideas in this section, and from there, you can start imagining which ones you like.

- **Eat healthy foods and take some vitamins.** Your mental health and diet are intertwined. Consuming fast foods and sugars increases your risk of depression. Moderation!

- **Move.** If you are depressed, you may not want to get up or exercise, but that is what you need the most. Find a way to be active that feels good to you.

- **Use your phone to enforce your positive habits.** Set alarms or reminders to help you complete the daily activities you pick as part of your routine.

- **Drink plenty of water.** According to a study published by the *World Journal of Psychiatry*, drinking water can reduce depression.

- **Practice mindfulness, meditation, and journaling.** One time a day from five to ten minutes suffices!

- **Soak up the sun.** Vitamin D is one of the best ones to combat depression.

- **Be grateful.** Practicing gratitude reminds you how good it is to see another person smile.

- **Time management.** Get a planner or use your phone but get organized!

- **Practice sleep hygiene.** Go to bed at any time that is good for you but sleep enough hours to feel rested. Set a daily routine you can practice at least fifteen minutes before you turn the lights off.

When creating your positivity routine, use some of these ideas and explore your own.

THE SITUATION: You've been feeling lethargic, and the lack of energy prevents you from doing much. You can see that you have things to do but it is difficult for you to muster up interest. If you're not proactive, the symptoms and the list of things to do will increase, making it challenging for you to catch up. You want to stay on top of your routine but wonder how to do so.

QUICK TIP: Get a pen and paper and list the things you have to do and how it would benefit you to complete those tasks or responsibilities. If you cannot leave the bed or chair, just make mental notes of what I just mentioned. Pick only one of the items you thought of or wrote about and review again how completing just that one thing benefits you. Then, trying to stick to your routine, do that one task that same day, leaving the rest for later or the next day. Addressing one thing at a time can help you get back to your routine and regain your energy.

MENTAL HEALTH JOURNAL

Now that you have designed your own positivity routine, you can start using it and making sure that it becomes a regular practice. An excellent way to ensure you stick to your practice is to reflect on how, when, and why you will do each element of your routine. Doing this will get your thoughts and plan in order, helping you achieve your goals and enhancing your sense of well-being and self-esteem.

Use the space to practice your journaling skills. Share how you plan to stick to your routine and incorporate a plan B for days when you may need to be flexible. Also, write when you will perform each activity and why you think it will benefit you.

When you are done, read what you wrote and make any necessary corrections to ensure you follow your plan.

How do you plan to reward yourself daily, weekly, or monthly for sticking to your routine?

TAILORING YOUR DAYS

Now that you know what a positivity routine is and its benefits, you can envision what yours would look like. The easiest way to begin designing one is brainstorming some ideas, somewhat like a rough draft or list. From there, you can create a more elaborate or complete plan. Be creative and have fun!

Go over each of the following prompts and complete the sentence with an idea for your positivity routine. There is no right or wrong, only what you like and what works for you.

Ex: I can treat myself ... by eating my favorite foods throughout the week.

1. Instead of overthinking, I will _____.

2. Starting my day with an affirmation helps me _____.

3. An activity I can do every morning to start a good day is _____

_____.

4. A good habit I can start is _____.

5. I can practice gratitude every day by _____.

6. Writing can help me _____.

7. I will drink more water to be _____.

8. I will listen to some music, including _____.

9. I will practice mindfulness by _____.

PAUSE AND REFLECT

You did it again! You are done with week 6 and that means another goal met. Congratulations! This week, you learned about defusion and positivity routines and how they benefit your mental and emotional health. How do you think you will implement these two in your daily life? As you reflect, remember that practice is essential to not forgetting what you have learned. Throughout this week, you brainstormed ideas to create a plan for your daily routine. How easy or challenging was that? What do you need in order to finish that plan or keep it up to date?

You can go back and review the material covered this week if you have any questions, but I imagine you also remember plenty of what you practiced. One of the main questions I have for you is: How can you stick to your positivity routine for at least fifteen days? It is doable; you just have to use the information you learned here and review it as often as you need. You are the director of this project, and you can go at your own pace. Never forget that!

Key Takeaways

- Cognitive defusion helps you detach from your negative thoughts. Positivity is about seeing the good side of things and being optimistic the majority of the time—even when you do not believe it. Your positive thoughts become your reality.

- Your mind plays tricks on you, inviting you to overthink. Focus on your strengths, following your routines, and positivity. Reframe!

- You are in control of what you think and how you behave.

- You know the benefits of sticking to a routine and will do a fantastic job creating and following yours.

Facing Your Fears

In this chapter, you will learn about facing and accepting your fears, which is one of the main alternatives to avoidance. It involves embracing any past and any current events that cause discomfort and fear. This can include depressive symptoms, like choosing to go out when you do not feel like it. For example, when you feel very depressed and do not want to deal with it, acceptance invites you to embrace the feelings so that you can process them. As you go through this chapter, and practice exposure, remind yourself that you know how to engage in reframing and acceptance. You will also need to remember to be flexible. If something is too challenging, use your tools to help you face your fears. You've got this!

I have the power to change my
thoughts and face my fears.
I'm strong. I'm in charge.

CHECKING IN

Last week, you practiced positivity and cognitive defusion. Both help you detach from your negative thoughts. By now, you know that positivity is about seeing the good side of things. The main idea is not to allow the negative thoughts to stay in your mind and create a mountain of doubt and negativity. Since your mind likes to play tricks, making you overthink, you have to stop it from taking the lead. You are in control, so focus on your strengths!

In this activity, you will practice positivity by writing about yourself. Describe your thoughts or your day, then practice changing all the ideas you can think of into positive ones.

Example: If you think, *I do not know what to write*, the positive translation will be: *Writing the letter will require an effort, but it is doable. I do not know what to write, but I will start with one sentence and will change it as needed.*

After you are done, read your letter. Circle or underline the positive ideas you find. You are able to think positively, and even just one example counts.

Moving Beyond Your Comfort Zone

This chapter will help you address fear in a safe and supportive way through slow exposure. It does not have to happen overnight. Fear is an overwhelming feeling caused by worry, and it can prevent you from taking an action that you want to perform. The more you worry, the worse the fear becomes, generating procrastination or total avoidance. To be able to reach your goals, you must face your fears. Functioning outside of your comfort zone requires practice and tools, both of which you will acquire throughout this chapter. In therapy, we refer to "slow exposure" as systematic desensitization, and it combines relaxation techniques with gradual exposure to help you slowly overcome your fears. In the beginning, it may not be easy to face your fears, but the more you practice it in a self-caring way, the easier it will become.

ADDRESSING FEAR

When I was young, I was afraid of the dark. As an adult, that fear and many of my childhood fears disappeared. As you grow, the brain develops and adapts to new situations, allowing you to let go of some emotions or thoughts. Some are negative, and if this negativity is fed, the fear becomes persistent. Many times, overcoming fear is accomplished by reminding the brain that you are in control and practicing positive thinking techniques. This is called psychological flexibility, the practice of being in the here and now and not being overly reactive to our negative thoughts.

Everyone experiences insecurities when leaving their comfort zone. Avoidant places we have created can be challenging to reenter, but it's doable. Real fears (things that actually happen, like trauma) or imaginary fears (things that have not happened, but we have worried into reality) produce unwanted thoughts. But no matter which type of fear it is, you can control your mind and how you react. Addressing insecurities is one of this week's goals. This will be a big step in moving past fears, both real and imagined. Use your tools and the strategies I have shared to tackle your fears:

1. Practice your breathing exercises (see page 27).

2. Look at the evidence.

3. Do not allow perfectionism to take the lead.

4. Face your fears slowly, one day at a time.

5. Use your happy place (see page 117).

6. Write about your fear as if you were describing it to someone you trust.

7. Practice mindfulness and ground yourself (see page 97).

EXPOSURE INTERVIEW

When you experience fear, your mind can also create negative thoughts that trigger you or make you think about something you want to avoid, like being chased or made fun of. When you take the time to address those fearful thoughts, you take away the power they have over you, and you take control of how you feel.

Answer the following questions as if you were interviewing yourself. Do not think too much about the answers; there is no right or wrong. Just write the first answer that comes to mind.

Write about a fear that you last experienced.

What did you feel? Describe it in detail.

In what part(s) of your body do you feel it?

How is it on a scale of 1 to 10, with 1 being mild and 10 severe?

Now allow yourself to re-create that feeling and experience whatever it is you are currently feeling without avoiding it. What are you thinking? How does it feel?

Are your thoughts and feelings facts, or are you making assumptions about the fear?

Experiencing and accepting your fear, and unwanted thoughts that come with it, allows you to practice exposure and process it. You just did. Use these questions to address unwanted thoughts.

NAMING YOUR FEAR

Recognizing that fear affects you in one or more ways can help you normalize the feelings that come with it. However, to accept it, more effort is needed. This activity can take you a step further in practicing that acceptance.

This activity can be completed sitting or lying down or walking inside or outside the house.

Wherever you are, take a few moments to think about fears that you experienced during the past week or so.

When you identify the fear, give it a name, like "Angry Visitor."

After you label it, voice or write down how it makes you feel when you experience it. Let it know that you allow it to be present, but you also know it always goes back to where it came from. This time will not be the exception.

Allow it to wait outside your body. Imagine leaving it in one of the rooms where you just were or simply send it outside. Let it know it has to remain there or leave, but it cannot get back inside you.

Continue with your daily activities, and when you think about the fear, repeat that you accept that it is there, but it does not have the power to bother you. You are in control.

This exercise can be practiced as many times as you want.

REVISIT GOALS AND VALUES

When I meet with my clients in session, we talk about their goals, ideas, or projects that have an endpoint, and we also discuss values, which usually last a lifetime. In a previous chapter, you worked with your values (see page 54). Today, you will revisit them along with your goals, such as finishing a project.

In therapy, we frequently refer to values as chosen life directions; activities that define you, describe you, or give your life meaning; or things you are known for or will be remembered for. Therapists typically compare values to a compass because they provide you with direction and guide you throughout your ongoing journey. For example, if you value compassion, you direct yourself to be kind to others, help them when they need it, and be there for them if they are struggling. That is your direction. Everyone has different values, and they can change over time, depending on the needs of the person. Another way to identify your values is by thinking about the answers to the following questions: What do you want your life to be about? What do you want to do that you cannot do because of the depression? What truly matters to you? It's all about you.

Now take a moment to reflect on these questions: What are the activities/goals you've been avoiding? What would take you outside your comfort zone while still being safe and supportive?

You can write down your answers using the provided space. Then rank your top three. You will use those top three picks later this week.

DESIGNING YOUR GOAL

Using SMART to define your goals is more effective than other goal-setting activities because it provides structure. As we discussed in week 1, SMART is an acronym that stands for specific, measurable, attainable, relevant, and time-bound. Use this space to formulate a SMART goal.

SPECIFIC: Name precisely what you want to achieve.

My goal is

MEASURABLE: What will serve as evidence that I have completed my goal?

I will track the progress toward my goal by

ATTAINABLE: Is my goal truly realistic, considering costs, time, and effort?

My goal is attainable because I can

RELEVANT: Is my goal important to me?

Achieving this goal is meaningful to me because

TIME-BOUND: What realistic but flexible deadlines will you follow?

I will achieve my goal by, or my deadlines are

REVIEWING MY VALUES

Values are guiding personal beliefs without an endpoint. Complete the following chart to explore values in different areas of your life.

Emotional: *(Ex: care, kindness, love)*
Physical: *(Ex: fitness, strength)*
Occupational: *(Ex: advancement, recognition, creativity)*
Intellectual: *(Ex: learning, knowledge, challenge)*
Social: *(Ex: cooperation, connection, adventure)*
Financial: *(Ex: security, stability, freedom)*
Moral: *(Ex: responsibility, punctuality, respect)*
Environmental: *(Ex: consciousness, volunteerism)*

Quick Tip: Combining Your Goals and Values

THE SITUATION: You are having a good day and want to take advantage of it. You sit or lie down and start writing down your goals and how your values can help you accomplish them. When you finish, you see the lists, but you don't know how to combine them or what to do next. You can clearly differentiate what they are, but you can't determine the next step.

QUICK TIP: Separate each goal and write down one or more values next to it (*Ex: Eat healthier: creativity by designing a meal plan or changing ingredients*). Then write down how you can be more creative with your meals. Perhaps by looking online or by asking a friend who cooks.

Taking the First Step

Taking the first step to do something we are afraid of can be daunting. You may think about past experiences or worry about the result. However, you cannot live in the past or be anxious about the future; you must live in the present. You can make that first step more manageable by creating an action plan. For example, the plan could be related to participating in social activities you have avoided in the past out of fear. Planning can be the first step to feeling more comfortable in social situations, and it can help you practice psychological flexibility or living in the present. I will show you how to use slow exposure to accomplish this as you develop your plan.

To increase psychological flexibility, you must pay close attention to the present and use your goals and values. Think of your goal, and again match it to your values.

DEVELOP YOUR PLAN

Slow exposure can help you overcome fears in a number of social situations. I will help you work on that action plan in the following weeks, so you can try incorporating slow exposure and developing your plan at home. The two most important considerations when getting started are appreciating that you must work at your own pace and understanding your motivations to act now.

In avoiding potentially unpleasant situations, it feels like you're reducing your stress and protecting yourself. However, this is a short-term solution that it is not recommended because getting accustomed to handling your triggers and fears is the best way to build resilience and reach your goals. You should create a plan to gradually introduce yourself to the feared situation, slowly increasing your participation into more complex ones. The plan includes staying exposed to the fear until it diminishes. This kind of exposure training can be practiced in your imagination first and then in real situations or what we know in therapy as *in vivo*. For example, you can start imagining getting ready to participate in a social event. Observe how you feel even if uncomfortable, then stop. Imagine yourself attending the social event now that you've visualized preparing for it. As you start experiencing the fear, use your breathing techniques and picture finding a friend that makes you feel safe. Then imagine your friend stepping out while you stay alone. Then visualize your friend returning to sit next to you. Stop and practice again tomorrow.

PROGRESSIVE RELAXATION

This method of deep relaxation is based on the idea that muscle tension is the body's psychological response to unwanted thinking. This exercise is an excellent way to reduce fear when confronting uncomfortable situations. You can practice this physically or just visualize yourself doing it while sitting or lying own. Take your time to feel each body part and slowly move into the next one until you are done. Use your 4-7-8 breathing technique between sets of this activity.

1. **Hands.** Make fists with both hands and open and close them.

2. **Arms.** Tense your arms as if you were trying to show your muscles.

3. **Eyes.** Raise your eyebrows as high as they will go.

4. **Mouth.** Open your mouth as wide as you can. Pretend to yawn.

5. **Neck.** Move your head to one side like trying to touch your shoulders with it.

6. **Shoulders.** Lift your shoulders up and then down. Relax.

7. **Chest.** Breathe in as deep as you can, hold for a count of seven, then exhale.

   Repeat each body part set as many times as you feel comfortable.

TURNING IDEAS INTO ACTION

It is your turn to choose one activity or goal to try this week. It can be related to something you want to do or something that causes fear, practicing slow exposure.

To turn ideas into action, you can use the ideation process. It has three easy steps to follow: capture, develop, and act.

The capture step involves you writing the activity or goal in your notebook so you do not forget about it. Having a notebook or journal for this purpose can make it even more powerful. Sometimes it can be challenging to name a goal because we fear that the next step will require an effort. Do not think about what comes next; just write your idea down and close your notebook.

Developing is about taking the first step to map or design your idea. Take a day or more to work on it but have a timeline. You want to be as specific as possible. Remember SMART goals? Use the method here. Be descriptive; by developing what you will do as clearly as possible, you avoid wasting efforts in the future.

Finally, act on the idea. Remind yourself you came up with the idea; since you planned this very *carefully*, the fear element is reduced to a minimum. Be consistent and detailed while completing the action, and reward yourself when you complete it.

Document your progress and reflections on the lines provided.

Quick Tip: Create Your Space

THE SITUATION: At home, you find yourself wanting to work on developing your goals, selecting more values, or your action plan. You know what steps to follow but find it challenging to start or finish because you get distracted or experience difficult emotions.

QUICK TIP: Find an area in your home where you can create your personal space. It can be in the corner of a room, your desk, couch, or bed. Have a plant or a candle, some music or rain sounds, and use pillows or a small blanket. Make the space your own just for your personal growth.

PRACTICING EXPOSURE TO PREPARE FOR PLANNING

Use the following exercise to continue practicing exposure so you can feel more at ease when working on your goals and action plan. By addressing your fears with this exercise, you are exposing yourself to them in a safe way, writing in your workbook. By the time you start creating your action plan in the future, and think about your fears there, you will feel more comfortable since you faced your fears here first.

One of my fears is:

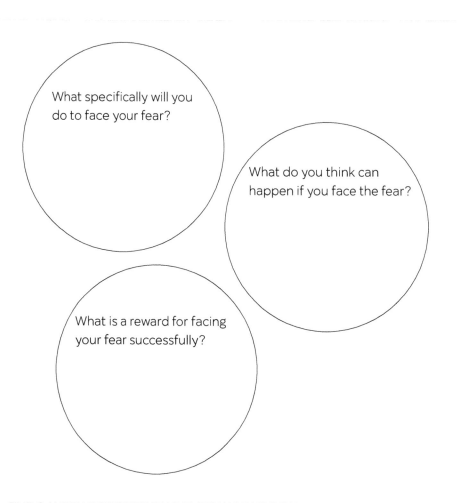

After you finish answering the questions in the circles, ask yourself:

Was I able to face my fear? What did I learn from this activity?

What evidence do I have that I can handle the situation successfully?

PAUSE AND REFLECT

This chapter was about facing and accepting your fears. You learned that your mind can exacerbate them, but you can use your tools to control them. Reflect on what tools you've gained and how you can use them to control those fears. You learned about positivity earlier, and this week taught you about acceptance. Which of the two work better for you? Are there specific situations in which you might rely on positivity and others situations better suited for acceptance? You also practiced embracing your history and any current experiences that cause discomfort due to unprocessed fear. Was this challenging? If so, what did you do to diminish the discomfort? If it was not challenging, what did you learn or like about embracing uncomfortable situations or emotions?

It is so rewarding to see you get to this point. You are only a few days away from completing this journey. Before you start your next week, reflect on what you have learned this week as a whole. What worked or didn't work? Last, think about the areas where you have seen more growth, and the areas that are still works in progress.

Key Takeaways

- Accepting your fears involves embracing your history and any current experiences that cause discomfort due to fear.

- Moving outside your comfort zone requires you to do it in a safe and supportive way.

- Psychological flexibility is the practice of being in the present and not overly reactive to our negative thoughts.

- You cannot live in the past or be anxious about the future; you must live in the present.

- The ideation process technique helps you turn ideas into action, and it has three easy steps to follow: capture, develop, and act.

WEEK 8

Bringing It All Together

I am very proud of you for accomplishing so much. It is not an easy task to stay committed, and you did it! When you read the material this week and complete the exercises, do it at your own pace and go back to previous chapters if you need to. This is not to prepare for a test but to ensure you master what you learned to use it in your everyday life.

Taking care of yourself and your emotional health is an essential task. Pay close attention to your strengths and weaknesses and those topics you found especially challenging during the past weeks. This is the last week of your practice but also an invitation to continue using what you have learned.

Reaching my small goals brings me closer to accomplishing the bigger ones. I am stronger than any depression symptom.

CHECKING IN

During the previous weeks, you covered a myriad of information. Some of those basic concepts will be used in this chapter and for weeks to come as you practice what you learned. Here is some information for you to review. Complete the following exercise by connecting the term with its description using lines.

A. Psychological flexibility	1.	A mood disorder characterized by an ongoing loss of interest and feeling of sadness, which can interfere with your daily functioning.
B. Positivity	2.	The practice of being in the present and not overly reactive to our negative thoughts.
C. Depression	3.	Seeing life through a positive lens.
D. Evidence-based therapy	4.	Skills and practices you keep in a handy tool kit to control depression.
E. Wellness tools	5.	Chosen life directions; activities that define you, describe you, or give your life meaning; or things you are known for or will be remembered for.
F. Values	6.	Changing a negative thought into a positive one.
G. Cognitive defusion	7.	A technique that involves learning how to separate from your thoughts by taking a step back and being an observer.
H. Reframing	8.	Any type of therapy that has been demonstrated to be scientifically valid or effective.
I. Coping mechanisms	9.	Tactics or strategies you use to protect yourself and reduce unpleasant emotions during difficult times.

How did you do? Check your responses using the key below:

A.2, B.3, C.1, D.8, E.4, F.5, G.7, H.6, I.9

Where Are You Now?

You have come a long way in learning about depression, its symptoms, and the tools to feel better. It is now time to reflect on your progress since you began this workbook.

Within the last seven weeks, you have learned that depression is a mood disorder that causes an ongoing loss of interest and feeling of sadness, which can interfere with your daily functioning. Through the readings, exercises, and self-reflection, you have also learned how it affects you personally. You experienced potentially difficult feelings while addressing your own challenges, learning new tools, and seeking personal growth. Those feelings may have been doubt, concern, fear, and even disbelief. However, as you continued advancing, those thoughts dissipated, and you got to where you are now. Ask yourself about your personal growth and how it has changed from the day you started this book until today. You have committed to addressing your mental health and doing the challenging work, and you have grown emotionally.

You also dealt with the feelings caused by having to complete activities and practices such as breathing techniques, worksheets, and reframing. Think about how you will incorporate these practices to help you in the future. You also practiced acceptance, living in the present, and changing your negative thoughts. Reflect on what you have learned from this process.

You have accomplished so much. Congratulations on getting here today! You have shown interest, commitment, and perseverance. How do you feel about what you've learned in the past weeks? What achievement makes you feel the happiest? Proudest? This is only the beginning of many more opportunities to achieve your goals. Remind yourself of all you have achieved when you initiate a new project or set a new goal, or even when you need motivation to keep going.

The learning opportunities in this workbook gave you a sense of how it feels to be mindful, reframe, and accept. Now you will have the chance to take those tools into your everyday life and practice what you find most useful. Each piece of information you acquired here added to your knowledge and your wellness tool kit.

Every new beginning has its challenges, and this was likely no different. When you decided to open this workbook, perhaps some days were easier than others or some of the exercises were more relevant than others. But you managed to complete all of them. What did you find challenging? How did you manage to overcome it and continue?

Quick Tip: Quieting Your Self-Critic

THE SITUATION: You have been thinking about working on a goal. All week you've felt energized. However, on Saturday morning, you wake up not wanting to leave your room or work on your goal. That creates more negative feelings. Your mind and self-critic tell you negative things about yourself. But you remember you can reframe or accept those thoughts.

QUICK TIP: Reframe by thinking about something you accomplished in the past. *Example: I'm committed.* Or accept that it's just your brain creating that inner negative voice, not you. Practice your journaling to write about your strengths or past accomplishments.

LETTING GO OF YOUR NEGATIVE THOUGHTS

Letting go is a process that frees you from negative thoughts and unwanted feelings. It is a skill that one can practice and master over time. You can let your negative thoughts go by paying attention to your surroundings and then practicing acceptance. For example, you can practice this mindfulness activity to quiet your thoughts for a short period of time, then repeat an accepting affirmation.

For this activity, sit or lie down, stand up, or walk around while you visualize or look for shapes. For example, look around the room or in your mind for something that looks like a rectangle, a circle, a square, etc. Most likely, you will recognize those shapes if there is a door, window, painting, or picture. Take one or two minutes, concentrating on what you are seeing or feeling. When you are done, come up with an affirmation practicing acceptance. For example, *I quieted my mind thanks to this exercise, now I accept that I have to continue with my activities.* Now take a deep breath, pick another shape, and do it again. When you are done, think about one item you just recognized. As you connect with your surroundings while practicing letting go and acceptance, you are defusing your thoughts and being in the present.

DEFUSING NEGATIVE THOUGHTS

Questioning if something is true or just a thought helps us recognize that thoughts are not facts. When you question, you are being mindful. This activity will guide you through cognitive defusion as a mindfulness activity.

Visualize yourself letting negative thoughts go; your mind created them, and they are no longer valid. When you are done, write down each negative thought inside the circle and scratch it out until you cannot see it. Scribbling or scratching out is another tool you can place in your wellness tool kit.

Think about a time when you had a negative thought that made you feel worried, even though you had no proof that it was true. For example, *No one wants to spend time with me.* Or *I do not do anything right.*

As you acknowledge your negative thoughts, ask yourself the following questions:

- Is that a thought or a fact?

- What evidence do I have other than thinking about it or sensing it? If I asked a person that cares about me if this were true, what would they say?

Take some time to reflect on your answers.

ACCEPTING THE UNWANTED

Often unwanted things happen, and we have no control over a specific situation. We cannot change people's behaviors or the reality of what is happening, and these experiences can be painful. The option you have at that point is to accept. Acceptance involves agreeing to something. Radical acceptance is about acknowledging that something happened and was real. Practicing radical acceptance will help you evaluate problems and reduce the emotional charge of the situation.

Use the following prompts to help you practice acceptance:

Find. What is a situation that has bothered you within the last twelve months? (For example, think about a time when you were not invited or selected to do something, and you felt left out.)

Ask. Is the situation something you have control over or can change? If it is, how can you change this reality? If not, what can you do about it?

Accept. Can you accept it in your thoughts? What will happen if you don't?

Process. You have allowed yourself to accept what happened and how you felt, acknowledging that something happened and was real. How are you feeling after you accepted the situation?

Looking Ahead

Depression is a complex condition, and treating it involves changing how you approach stressors, improving coping mechanisms, and increasing your resilience. Although depression may not be defeated, remember that it can be managed, and you have the strategies and resources to do that.

Now that you have worked through weeks of information and exercises, ask yourself this: *What did I accomplish because of the work I put into this workbook?* You have indeed accomplished so much. All the material you learned will be with you for years to come. You can implement these skills in your everyday life by reframing when negative thoughts attack or when you want to create a plan of action to reach your goals. And those are just some examples, since you will be able to do much more thanks to the skills you have acquired and will maintain. You are now more resilient and have the power to change unwanted situations. You are the one in charge because you have the knowledge and the tools to succeed. As often as you can, think about your needs and be open and kind when you do that. You want to continue taking care of yourself and do even more wonderful things after completing this book.

To create a plan as you move forward, you may want to choose topics from this workbook that you found most helpful and integrate those into your daily activities. You might decide to set ten or fifteen minutes a day to review what you have learned or to work on your plans or goals. If you have a set of goals in your mind, that could be a great start. Use them, and keep in mind you have the tools to organize your ideas. This is also a good opportunity for you to brainstorm and find additional goals. For each goal, you can create a plan. It can be daily, weekly, monthly, etc. You are the leader of this venture!

Also, remember to use your inner power daily. Think about ways to continue feeling motivated. If you need help with motivation, think about three or five things that make you happy and write them down. For example, *feeling better,* or *being able to be more social.* Then you can place them where you can see them every day. Most of all, motivate yourself by thinking about how far you have gotten. I am very proud of you!

Quick Tip: Staying on Track

THE SITUATION: You have the intention to continue to practice what you learned. The interest is there, but life happens, and you have other responsibilities to attend to, leaving you little or no time to work on your goals.

QUICK TIP: Set a specific time that works for you during the day. It doesn't have to be at the beginning or end of the day. If you need to, do it during one of your breaks or while you eat; set three- to five-minute "me sessions" to avoid feeling overwhelmed at the end of the day or when you need to do something pressing in the morning.

MY PERSONAL PLAN

What areas do I need to work on?

My main goal for this week is

One thing I need to do to live a happier or more satisfying life is

Three of the most important things I must do this week to achieve this are

_____

_____

_____

_____

Two values I can use to help me reach my goal are _____

_____

One person I can talk to about this goal and feel motivated about it is

_____

One thing I am going to do today to get me closer to my goal is

_____

_____

One thing I can do to reward myself after I accomplish my goal is

_____

_____

_____

At the end of each week, complete a check-in by taking some time to write and evaluate if you accomplished your one goal and how easy or difficult it was. If you did accomplish it, reward yourself, and then pick another goal to complete the following week. You can do this every week. Start with small goals and gradually increase the level of difficulty or length of time required to complete your plan. You can use a calendar to set a reminder at the end of each week to check how you did.

REUSABLE PLANNING WORKSHEET

You can make copies of this page to use during future weekly planning sessions. The more you practice, the easier it will be to complete them as the worksheets become a natural part of your routine.

My weekly goal is:

My priorities are:

The values I can use are:

The steps I can take to accomplish my goal are:

My support system (people I can share my goals with or reach out to if I need help):

After completing my goal, I can reward myself with:

STEP-BY-STEP TOWARD MY GOALS

Identifying the steps you can take to help you get closer to your goals doesn't have to be complicated. When a goal is close to your heart, it becomes easier to accomplish. You can use your SMART goals tool (specific, measurable, attainable, relevant, and time-bound) to make it easier for you to plan those goals. It is important to set realistic steps, which you can accomplish by dividing goals into small tasks that you will complete using a timeline. (Example: Organizing a closet, starting with the shoes then the bottoms.) As you commit to following the steps, you'll put into practice what you have learned these past seven weeks.

In the space provided, list the steps you plan to take to stay motivated and avoid procrastination, fear, or perfectionism.

Ex: During the week, I will set aside ten minutes as often as I can to work on my goal.

1. _____

2. _____

3. _____

4. _____

5. _____

What can you do if you encounter difficulties along the road?

_____

_____

What can you use from your wellness tool kit to stay on track?

_____

_____

_____

When to Seek Help

Before you move on, it is important to mention that relapse can be a part of recovery, and if you do not see the improvement you expected, it may be necessary to seek professional help. Whether you have already dealt with these issues for a long time, or a voice is telling you that you do not want to feel the way you feel anymore, any reason you feel motivated to seek support is valid. Remember, you do not need to wait to be in crisis to seek help.

Asking for support can be daunting, and lots of people fear voicing their need due to stigma. First of all, it is okay to ask for help. Know that it is not a sign of weakness, but one of courage and commitment, to want to feel better. You'll discover that there are various resources to choose from, and you will be able to select the one that works best for you. You can talk to your primary doctor or look online for resources in your community. Another way to ask for support is by contacting a friend, teacher, coworker, or family member you trust. You do not have to share the situation or specific problems if you do not want to. You can just ask them for recommendations to find a mental health professional.

If you are experiencing a crisis, contact 911 or a mental health hotline immediately. Many of these hotlines provide services and have counselors that can talk to you and answer any questions you may have regarding your mental health.

Understanding the way each type of therapy can benefit you is worth some research. According to the American Psychological Association, group therapy is helpful if sharing in company and being around individuals who have similar experiences makes you feel more comfortable addressing your fears. Some therapists focus on you and your environment, others focus on you the individual. Psychiatrists can prescribe medication if necessary. There are in-person or telehealth considerations as well. Do the research, and make sure you select what is best for you. Last, know that you aren't stuck forever with a particular therapist or type of therapy. Explore your options.

Remember that when asking for help, you are taking care of yourself. You're showing that you're strong and brave. It's empowering. It's healthy. It may be hard, but it's worth it.

Continuing the Momentum

As you reach the end of this workbook, take a moment to reflect on every piece of knowledge you acquired. Congratulate yourself! I am delighted to see you got to this point. We walked together, and now it is time for you to keep going. I genuinely hope you continue practicing and using every tool shared in this workbook.

Your wellness tool kit and every tool inside it will help you work with your negative thoughts and emotions, modifying your feelings and actions. Reflect on your stress management techniques, such as the 4-7-8 breathing exercise, journaling, and body scanning. You also have a reusable worksheet you can print and use often. Your recovery is a personal growth process, so what you are doing is all for you. The skills and tools you have learned here will accompany you for life.

If at any point you feel like you are relapsing or not following your plan as intended, use your values and rewards system. Look for new motivators, and remember you have the power to stay emotionally and mentally healthy. Relapse is another opportunity to start and succeed, so be kind to yourself if you are not where you want to be. Celebrate your milestones.

Remember, you have the power to create change and continue practicing your skills. When needed, return to the parts of the book that may have caused confusion during the eight weeks. The work that you have done is about improving life—it's not either/or and it's not time-bound. It's a gesture of self-love (and more!) to take care of yourself. I hope that this workbook gave you not only the tools but also the interest and motivation to continue taking care of yourself daily. I wish you all the best and know that you will do your best to face challenging situations using the material you learned here. During the next eight weeks, and for the rest of your life, remember, you have the tools and skills you need; use them. You are in control!

PAUSE AND REFLECT

Take some time to write about your big accomplishment and how you feel about it, including some of the things you learned these past eight weeks and how your journey was. You have done a truly amazing job and stayed strong, so this will be an opportunity to share your thoughts about it.

When you finish, read what you wrote and reflect on it.

Key Takeaways

- To reach your goals, you have to face them and use the tools you have learned.

- Practicing what you learned will allow you to gain more confidence.

- You can continue taking care of yourself and your emotional health by paying special attention to your strengths and weaknesses.

- Relapse can be a part of recovery, so if you do not see improvement, it may be necessary to contact a professional to ask for help.

- Do not forget to celebrate your milestones.

- You have shown interest, motivation, commitment, and perseverance. Continue using your learned skills in the future.

Resources

WEBSITES

Anxiety and Depression Association of America, adaa.org/supportgroups
The ADAA website offers information to find support groups in the nation. Joining a support group is beneficial to share and learn from others' experiences.

Monday Mandalas, mondaymandala.com/m
This is a website with coloring sheets to download and print. Coloring is a great way to explore mindfulness creatively.

National Institute of Mental Health, nimh.nih.gov/health/publications/depression
The NIMH website offers a myriad of information and resources to educate ourselves and others about mental health conditions.

National Suicide Prevention Lifeline,
suicidepreventionlifeline.org/talk-to-someone-now
This lifeline offers emotional support to people of all ages. It is available 24/7 across the United States. It is open to everyone, accessible, and confidential.

Psychology Today, psychologytoday.com/us/therapists/depression
This website offers information about mental health professionals in your area. You can find a licensed and certified depression therapist and sort the results based on your needs and location.

Psychology Tools, psychologytools.com/resource/mindful-attention-audio
This website offers audio mindfulness activities for becoming more aware of one's thoughts and experiences and observing these as transient mental events.

SAMHSA National Helpline, samhsa.gov/find-help/national-helpline
The Substance Abuse and Mental Health Services Administration runs a free, confidential, 24/7, 365-day-a-year treatment referral service in English/Spanish for individuals and families facing mental and emotional disorders.

SAMHSA Services Locator, findtreatment.samhsa.gov
The Behavioral Health Treatment Services Locator is a confidential and anonymous source of information for persons seeking treatment facilities in the United States for mental health problems.

The Trevor Project, thetrevorproject.org/resources/article/resources-for -mental-health-support
The Trevor Project's website offers the LGBTQ+ community mental health resources, including links and services offered to LGBTQ+ and their allies.

VIDEOS

"Don't Suffer from Your Depression in Silence" by Nikki Webber Allen, ted.com/talks /nikki_webber_allen_don_t_suffer_from_your_depression_in_silence
This TED Talk addresses some of the issues communities of color experience in reference to mental health.

"Quit Depression and Negative Thinking with Tapping (Emotional Freedom Technique)" by Renee Millman, youtube.com/watch?v=CbAndzHgtNc
This video presents information on and a guided practice of the emotional freedom technique, which involves tapping your fingertips on specific meridian points to reduce depression and stress.

"The Samurai and the Fly," youtu.be/R5-HNXxc5kk
This short video invites you to reflect while practicing mindfulness.

"This Could Be Why You're Depressed or Anxious" by Johann Hari, ted.com /talks/johann_hari_this_could_be_why_you_re_depressed_or_anxious
In this TEDx Talk, the presenter shares information to combat depression, focusing on your unmet human needs, such as human connection.

BOOKS

52-Week Mental Health Journal: Guided Prompts and Self-Reflection to Reduce Stress and Improve Well-being by Cynthia Catchings
This journal offers short prompts to write and reflect on while working on self-care and stress reduction.

References

Association for Contextual Behavioral Science. "Exercises and Meditations." Accessed April 12, 2022. contextualscience.org/act_exercises.

Ben-Porath, Denise D. "Stigmatization of Individuals Who Receive Psychotherapy: An Interaction between Help-Seeking Behavior and the Presence of Depression." *Journal of Social and Clinical Psychology* 21, no. 4 (October 2002): 400–413, doi:10.1521/jscp.21.4.400.22594.

Choose Mental Health. "Depression: 16 Facts and Myths." Accessed April 30, 2022. choosementalhealth.org/depression-16-facts-and-myths.

Depression Treatment Program at Portland Psychotherapy. "ACT Treatment of Depression." Accessed April 22, 2022. portlanddepressiontreatment.com/act -treatment-of-depression/.

Gould, Madelyn S. et al. "National Suicide Prevention Lifeline: Enhancing Mental Health Care for Suicidal Individuals and Other People in Crisis." *Suicide and Life-Threatening Behavior* 42, no. 1 (February 2012): 22–35, doi:10.1111/j.1943-278x.2011.00068.x.

Guttmacher, Jonathan A., and Lee Birk. "Group Therapy: What Specific Therapeutic Advantages?" *Comprehensive Psychiatry* 12, no. 6 (November 1971): 546–556, doi:10.1016/0010-440x(71)90037-x.

Haghighatdoost, Fahimeh et al. "Drinking Plain Water Is Associated with Decreased Risk of Depression and Anxiety in Adults: Results from a Large Cross-Sectional Study." *World Journal of Psychiatry* 8, no. 3, (September 2018): 88–96. doi: 10.5498/wjp.v8.i3.88.

Hamilton, David. "6 Ways Your Brain Can't Distinguish Real from Imaginary." David R. Hamilton PhD. August 2, 2019. drdavidhamilton.com/6-ways-your-brain-cant -distinguish-real-from-imaginary.

Johnson, Ben. "Psychotherapy: Understanding Group Therapy." American Psychological Association. October 31, 2019. apa.org/topics/psychotherapy/group-therapy.

Mayo Clinic. "Seasonal Affective Disorder (SAD): Symptoms and Causes." Accessed April 30, 2022. mayoclinic.org/diseases-conditions/seasonal-affective-disorder /symptoms-causes/syc-20364651.

Morahan-Martin, Janet, and Colleen D. Anderson. "Information and Misinformation Online: Recommendations for Facilitating Accurate Mental Health Information Retrieval and Evaluation." *CyberPsychology & Behavior* 3, no. 5 (October 2000): 731–746, doi:10.1089/10949310050191737.

National Institute of Mental Health. "Depression." Accessed April 22, 2022. nimh.nih.gov/health/publications/depression.

Pike, Karen, and Ben Fletcher. "Changing People's Habits Is Associated with Reductions in Stress, Anxiety and Depression Levels." Do Something Different Ltd. February 2016. dsd.me/business/wp-content/uploads/sites/12/2016/08/WhitePaper_Habit-Change-Reduces-Stress.pdf.pdf.

Psychology Tools. "Mindful Attention (Audio)." Accessed May 2, 2022. psychologytools.com/resource/mindful-attention-audio.

Raven, Kathleen. "Stress, Anxiety, or Depression? Treatment Starts with the Right Diagnosis." Yale Medicine. May 21, 2020. yalemedicine.org/news/stress-anxiety-depression.

Sickel, Amy E., Jason D. Seacat, and Nina A. Nabors. "Mental Health Stigma Update: A Review of Consequences." *Advances in Mental Health* 12, no. 3 (December 2014): 202–215, doi:10.1080/18374905.2014.11081898.

Smith, Michael W. "Easy Habits That Can Improve Your Mental Health." WebMD. August 20, 2021. webmd.com/depression/ss/slideshow-easy-habits-improve-mental-health.

Substance Abuse and Mental Health Services Administration. "Behavioral Health Treatment Services Locator." Accessed April 22, 2022. findtreatment.samhsa.gov.

The Trevor Project. "Resources for Mental Health Support." Accessed May 2, 2022. thetrevorproject.org/resources/article/resources-for-mental-health-support.

Veterans Affairs. "Depression Treatment for Veterans." Accessed April 22, 2022. va.gov/health-care/health-needs-conditions/mental-health/depression.

Zhang, Chun-Qing et al. "Acceptance and Commitment Therapy for Health Behavior Change: A Contextually-Driven Approach." *Frontiers in Psychology* 8, no. 11 (January 2018). doi:10.3389/fpsyg.2017.02350.

Index

Acknowledgments

I want to thank my editors for their knowledge and guidance and the rest of my publishing team for working with me. Thanks to Mom and Chase, for your patience; Clarence for being close while far away; and all of you, dear patients, who have experienced depression and learned to take control of it.

About the Author

 **CYNTHIA V. CATCHINGS**, LCSW-S, LCSWC, CMHIMP, CFTP, is a psychotherapist in private practice, an adjunct professor at the University of Texas RGV, mental health consultant, and president of the NASW-DC chapter. She's the founder and executive director of the Women's Emotional Wellness Center and Consulting Firm, with offices in Texas, Virginia, and Maryland. She has traveled globally to conduct mental health research in over thirty-five countries. Connect with her online at WomensEmotionalWellnessCenter.com.

CPSIA information can be obtained
at www.ICGtesting.com
Printed in the USA
JSHW010352180922
30612JS00001B/1

9 781638 781585